THE HEDGEHOG'S BALLOON

NICK BUTTERWORTH

Collins
Picture Lions

Percy the park keeper looked up
from his work and gazed in wonder.
"Two red ones . . . a blue one . . . there's a
yellow one . . . and another blue one . . ."

This edition produced for The Book People Ltd.,
Hall Wood Avenue, Haydock, St. Helens, WA11 9UL

First published in hardback in Great Britain by HarperCollins Publishers Ltd in 1996
First published in Picture Lions in 1999
1 3 5 7 9 10 8 6 4 2
ISBN: 0 00 776982 2

Picture Lions is an imprint of the Children's Division, part of HarperCollins Publishers Ltd

The HarperCollins website address is www.harpercollinschildrensbooks.co.uk

Printed and bound in Thailand

Percy was counting balloons. "I wonder where they're coming from," he said to himself. "Somebody must have had a party."

He put down his trowel and wiped his hands.

"Well, if nobody wants them," he said, "I think I'll help myself."

Percy chased after
the balloons as
they floated past him
on the breeze.
It didn't take him
long to collect
as many as he
could carry.
He began
to walk back
towards his
hut, whistling
happily.

Suddenly, Percy stopped. He could hear a faint sound coming from a tree stump nearby. It was not a happy sound.

"Someone's crying," said Percy. "Oh dear." He let go of his balloons and hurried over to the stump.

Sitting on the tree stump, and looking very upset, was a hedgehog. Two mice were doing their best to comfort him.

"Goodness me," said Percy. "Whatever is the matter?"

"It's all these balloons," said the hedgehog.

Then, in between sniffs and sobs, he explained to Percy how he had always loved balloons. The trouble was that he could never have them because they would always burst on his spines.

"It's just not fair!" And the hedgehog burst into tears again.

"You poor thing," said Percy.
He tried to put his arm around
the hedgehog but took it away at once.
"Ouch," he said.

Then Percy took one of his thick
gardening gloves out of his pocket and
put it on. The hedgehog nestled into
his hand.

"I think everyone should be able to play with balloons," said Percy. "And that includes hedgehogs."

He put on the other glove and gently carried the hedgehog towards an old store shed. The two mice followed.

The mice watched Percy through the window. He set the hedgehog down on a workbench and then he took a tin from a shelf. He opened the lid.

"What's Percy doing?" said one of the mice. "What's in that box?"

"I don't know," said the other mouse. "I can't see properly."

The mice didn't have to wait long to find out. Percy picked up the hedgehog and brought him outside.

"There!" said Percy. "A good idea, even if I say so myself! I think those balloons will be safe now."

The mice clapped and the hedgehog beamed. He thought how smart he must look, wearing his corks.

Percy caught hold of a bright yellow balloon.

"Here you are," said Percy as he handed it to the hedgehog. "Your very first balloon."

The hedgehog took the balloon and with a great big smile on his face, he scampered off with the balloon floating beside him.

"Another satisfied customer," said Percy, feeling pleased with himself.

Percy turned to go back to his hut. But suddenly, there came a loud BANG!

"Oops!" said Percy. "One of the corks must have come off. It's a good job we've got plenty of balloons!"

"Don't worry," Percy called to the hedgehog, "I'm coming..."

NICK BUTTERWORTH was born in North London
in 1946 and grew up in a sweet shop in Essex. He now lives
in Suffolk with his wife Annette and their two children,
Ben and Amanda.

The inspiration for the Percy the Park Keeper books
came from Nick Butterworth's many walks through the
local park with the family dog, Jake. The stories have sold
over two million copies and are loved by children all
around the world. Their popularity has led to the making
of a stunning animated television series, now available on
video from HIT Entertainment plc.

Introduction

GLOBAL CONFLICT is Volume 331 in the **ISSUES** series. The aim of the series is to offer current, diverse information about important issues in our world, from a UK perspective.

ABOUT GLOBAL CONFLICT

Global conflicts, some lasting just a few weeks, have left behind them many unexploded bombs, shells and land mines. Local communities have to live with the legacy they leave behind for many years afterwards. This book looks at current nuclear war threats and new technology used in modern-day warfare. It also looks at the victims who have to flee their homes and the effect this has on their lives. In addition to this, it considers the children caught up in conflict areas throughout the world.

OUR SOURCES

Titles in the **ISSUES** series are designed to function as educational resource books, providing a balanced overview of a specific subject.

The information in our books is comprised of facts, articles and opinions from many different sources, including:

⇨ Newspaper reports and opinion pieces

⇨ Website factsheets

⇨ Magazine and journal articles

⇨ Statistics and surveys

⇨ Government reports

⇨ Literature from special interest groups.

A NOTE ON CRITICAL EVALUATION

Because the information reprinted here is from a number of different sources, readers should bear in mind the origin of the text and whether the source is likely to have a particular bias when presenting information (or when conducting their research). It is hoped that, as you read about the many aspects of the issues explored in this book, you will critically evaluate the information presented.

It is important that you decide whether you are being presented with facts or opinions. Does the writer give a biased or unbiased report? If an opinion is being expressed, do you agree with the writer? Is there potential bias to the 'facts' or statistics behind an article?

ASSIGNMENTS

In the back of this book, you will find a selection of assignments designed to help you engage with the articles you have been reading and to explore your own opinions. Some tasks will take longer than others and there is a mixture of design, writing and research-based activities that you can complete alone or in a group.

Useful weblinks

www.actionaid.org.uk.

www.amnesty.org

www.belfasttelegraph.co.uk

www.child-soldiers.org

www.christianaidcollective.org

www.christianaid.org.uk

www.theconversation.com

defenceforchildren.org

www.handicap-international.org.uk

www.huffingtonpost.com

www.independent.co.uk

opinium.co.uk

www.oxfordresearchgroup.org.uk

www.politicshome.com

www.project-syndicate.org

www.redcross.org.uk

www.savethechildren.org.uk

www.scidev.net

www.sciencedaily.com

www.telegraph.co.uk

www.theguardian.com

www.unicef.org.uk

FURTHER RESEARCH

At the end of each article we have listed its source and a website that you can visit if you would like to conduct your own research. Please remember to critically evaluate any sources that you consult and consider whether the information you are viewing is accurate and unbiased.

Global Conflict

Editor: Tina Brand

Volume 331

Independence Educational Publishers

First published by Independence Educational Publishers

The Studio, High Green

Great Shelford

Cambridge CB22 5EG

England

© Independence 2018

ISBN-13: 978 1 86168 782 1

Printed in Great Britain

Zenith Print Group

Economic and viable warfare

Britain pledges £750 million to help improve the lives of Afghans following years of war

Exclusive: Aid will be focused on helping women and girls in the war-ravaged country.

Joe Watts, Political Editor

The UK will commit £750 million to help improve health, education and security in Afghanistan, under a major new funding announcement.

The money, welcomed by aid agencies on Saturday, is to be spent over three years and will have a particular focus on helping women and girls in the war-ravaged country.

Writing exclusively in *The Independent*, International Development Secretary Priti Patel said the boost would not only reduce misery and suffering in the world, but also serve Britain's interests by stabilising the country and reducing the need for people to make perilous long journeys to the UK.

It comes shortly after Theresa May travelled to the United Nations and the G20 to assure the world the UK would not turn in on itself following the Brexit vote, but also to urge leaders to do more to tackle mass-migration.

With the Conservative conference about to begin in Birmingham, Ms Patel also takes the opportunity to launch an attack on Labour claiming the party under Jeremy Corbyn is promoting socialist policies that held back global development for decades.

She said: "The UK's presence in Afghanistan over the last decade has helped improve security and prevent it from once again becoming a base of operations for global terrorists that would threaten the streets of Britain.

"We have improved the lives of Afghans significantly – with millions more children in school, better healthcare and greater prosperity. But huge challenges remain – not least the continuing threat from the Taliban.

"That is why the UK will commit up to £750 million, from the aid budget, to Afghanistan between 2017 and 2020 to help create a more stable country and improve people's lives – particularly for women and girls."

As well as spending on health and education services, the funding will contribute to the urgent UN flash appeal to help protect internally displaced people who have fled their homes, and clear land mines from areas where people live.

The HALO Trust, which helps to clear land mines and explosives said the funding is "very good news for the Afghan people".

Director of Communications Paul McCann said: "Decades of conflict has bequeathed Afghanistan a very large mines and explosive remnants of war problem, so this announcement from the UK Government is very welcome. It builds on Britain's strong commitment to mine clearance around the world.

"With funding, Afghanistan can be made mine-free. Already around 80 per cent of the country has been cleared – the job can be finished. Mozambique was made mine-free last year and it also had a huge problem.

"Mines and other explosive remnants of war maim and kill boys and girls,

men and women and hold back development. This is very good news for the people of Afghanistan."

Only last month a Taliban suicide attack near in Kabul killed at least 24 people and wounded 91 others. But despite security being a major problem in Afghanistan, aid agencies continue vital work.

Chair of Afghanaid Chris Kinder said: "We know, through over 30 years of experience, that this kind of sustained funding is essential to reach the most vulnerable individuals.

"Afghanaid's project, the Women's Economic Empowerment Programme, was launched in 2013. It delivers essential livelihood training, as well as literacy and business knowhow. The programme has reached over 14,000 women.

"Gender equality is the cornerstone of all Afghanaid projects. If we want to see long-term security and opportunity in Afghanistan, we must continue to invest in women's futures."

In her article, Ms Patel wrote that people in-part voted in the EU referendum for "a strong, independent Britain, able to shape our own destiny" and that addressing global challenges was an area where the aid budget had a crucial role to play.

She said: "People from Afghanistan make up a significant proportion of the migrant and refugee population entering Europe – nearly a quarter of those arriving in Greece by some estimates.

"As the Prime Minister made clear at the United Nations last month, our aid budget has a huge role to play in creating the jobs and economic opportunities that give people in the world's poorest countries a better alternative than risking the journey to Europe.

"In the long run, we will only stop people drowning in the Mediterranean if we tackle the instability that drives people to take such a risk."

In her piece she also condemns the recent bombing of an aid convoy in Syria, for which the West has accused Russia of being involved, which she called an "assault on our humanity".

Ms Patel recently committed Ms May's administration to spending 0.7 per cent of GDP on international aid, despite calls for the Government to drop the target.

Since coming into office she has demanded better transparency of aid funding and a reduction of waste, but an early commitment to use aid to boost trade, drew particular attacks from Labour.

Rounding on her political opponents, she said: "The tragic irony is that the Labour Party is now run by people who genuinely believe in the socialist policies which held back development and poverty reduction around the world in the last century – and whose consignment to history has allowed literally hundreds of millions of the world's most vulnerable people to escape poverty.

"But not only are they out of touch with economic reality. They are also out of touch with the concerns and interests of the British people – just as they are with so many other issues, from immigration to defence."

1 October 2016

⇨   The above information is reprinted with kind permission from *The Independent*. Please visit www.independent.co.uk for further information.

Is economic warfare the theme for 2015?

By Ambassador Muhamed Sacirbey

Is the Russian Ruble becoming financial rubble as consequence of targeting by the US and its allies? The dramatic fall in oil prices and commensurate drop in the Russian currency, is this coincidental to broader global economic trends or an orchestrated assault? Will economic warfare become the weapon of choice for 2015 as contrary agendas bring both old adversaries and some longer standing allies into conflict? The UN will be the forum for diplomatic debate where some sharp differences like a long submerged iceberg are now appearing above the surface of a new cold war, from Ukraine to Syria, to the East and South China Seas. However, the equity, debt, currency and commodity markets may be where the scores are settled.

Punishing Putin for Ukraine and Syria via oil trading and prices?

The drop in oil prices, as was its rapid rise over the last two decades, cannot be explained by fundamental economics of demand and supply. In part, the moves probably have been exaggerated by financial speculation. Banks and hedge funds have been players stampeding commodities markets, energy and other resources from metals to food stuffs. Gunvor, a Putin-associated energy 'trading firm' has long been connected with the rise of oil prices and with making the Russian strongman and his cronies billions in profits by effectively controlling that country's petroleum sales. Gunvor was one of the first targets of US and allied sanctions post Crimea annexation and Russia's continued intrusion into Ukraine.

Putin's effective manipulation of oil prices and self-enrichment may have been in part tolerated by multiple US administrations. Republicans saw it benefiting their oil constituency. Democrats saw higher petroleum costs as rationalising alternative energy as well as dampening fossil fuel demand and emissions. During both Republican and Democratic administrations dating back to the fall of the Berlin Wall there was also the vision, now more like a distant mirage, that Moscow would be a partner if not ally to the Euro-Atlantic democracies. Putin's abuses – from the suffocation of domestic opposition, to brutality in Chechnya, to bullying of neighbours – were tolerated in large part in the hope of co-opting the cooperation of the Russian regime. The sharp rise of energy was a costly premium to pay, but it allowed Putin to economically stabilise a deteriorating Russia, even if the base was not solid but rather fluid.

Paying for a resurrected 'imperial agenda'

The rise in oil and other commodities though also allowed Vladimir Putin to put into action a new imperial project. The invasions of Georgia and Ukraine are only the most visible of the effort for the Moscow leadership to reassert its influence on regional proxy despots and strongmen. The new riches had also facilitated Putin's narrative. He has deftly mixed windfall energy profits tossed at real economic pain and injured national pride with personality cult. However, with the illusion of new Moscow fading and the old Kremlin style reappearing, in Europe and Washington tolerance for Putin's excesses has also gone.

Saudi Arabia is the stick on Putin's donkey?

The role of Saudi Arabia in effectively talking prices down has been the topic of much speculation. Some attribute it to the world's largest oil producer's simple strategy of maintaining its share of the market by forcing other producers, OPEC and non, to decrease their production. Some though argue that this is a Saudi effort to subvert new US-based and higher cost-production including fracking. Others still see it as an economic assault upon competing regimes in Iran and Iraq.

Often there is no explicit 'conspiratorial' agreement, but in this instance there is an implicit understanding that US, EU and Saudi interests do converge particularly on punishing Putin for his support of the Assad Regime in the Syria conflict and diminishing the potential rise of a new axis that spans from Moscow to Caracas. US and Saudi interests converge more frequently than the rhetoric which makes OPEC and 'Arabs' convenient flogging targets in US domestic politics. Saudi Arabia has much to remedy in terms of its human rights standards. However, it has been a reliable Washington and EU ally as well as purchaser of consumer goods and weapons. Most critically from Riyadh's perspective, this is also an opportunity for Saudi Arabia to reassert its key global and regional role via its most effective diplomatic tool, oil and economic relevance.

Collateral damage

The drop in petroleum prices has also dragged down other commodities, including industrial metals. Again, keeping in mind that there is no perfect symmetry as in most conspiracy theories, some Euro-Atlantic allies as Australia, Canada and Mexico are being hurt disproportionately. Their economies in significant part are reliant upon natural resources. On the other hand, some other non-allies as China may substantially benefit. However, US, EU and Japanese economies will generally benefit while the rapid drop and particularly the painful adjustments will most hurt Russia, Venezuela, Iran and less transparent economies. Some of these regimes may need to seek IMF and/or World Bank relief. This will be another opportunity for the US and allies, whose influence is dominant in these international multilateral institutions, to discipline spendthrift regimes.

However, all may not be calm between the allies. Japan and Europe are caught in an extended downdraft. Depreciating the Yen appears a pillar of Tokyo's rehabilitation plan and may be ever more the remedy of choice for most European leaderships, with the notable exception of Germany and The Netherlands. The US may find its exports increasingly uncompetitive with a rising US Dollar. For this reason,

it has encouraged more structural changes and particularly moving toward growth inducements rather than the relatively unproductive austerity policy favoured by the Merkel-led government in Berlin. However, it is more likely that the very survival of the Eurozone (and the euro as currency) will be challenged from within by European governments as in Paris or Athens or in Rome or even the ECB (European Central Bank) who see a need for fiscal and monetary accommodation rather than staying the course of austerity which has long lost wind to its sails and direction to its rudder.

Swimming in a China sea

Conflicting claims to territorial seas/islands has pitted China against most of its neighbours. Military confrontation appeared almost inevitable before reason prevailed. The countries of South and East Asia including China are economically interdependent as markets and producers. The history of Japan–China conflict highlights a combustible nationalism that is frequently the pretext for competing for natural resources and regional economic influence. Beijing has sought to avoid multilateral institutions as the UN or the International Court of Justice to resolve such disputes and prefers bilateralism where it can employ its economic and military might to press smaller neighbours such as Vietnam or Malaysia. The scales of diplomatic might though have been at least in part tipped. The US has been invited into the jockeying by allies such as the Philippines. The regional economic and political regional association has also served to provide some balance. Nonetheless, China still dominates not only because of its rising military might but Chinese-dominated capital that defines fund flows throughout the region.

BRICS defined by economics not political alignment?

The BRICS (Brazil, Russia, India, China and South Africa) had been brought closer together by an emerging economic symbiosis but there may now be a further evolution and perhaps realignment of interests. The BRICS were defined by a status of emerging markets, both producers

of natural resources and consumers seeking accelerated industrialisation. As long as China was hungry for ores to oil, the economic interests were compatible, and, oh yes, the under-served markets of developing states in Africa and Asia were also particularly fertile for China-made products and investment.

At the UN though, the diverse diplomatic agenda of the BRICS was most notably sown together by an anti-US bias. This could perhaps be rationalised by a strategy to disrupt a uni-polar, Washington-dominated globe, particularly in the spirit of the 'Non-Aligned Movement' that evolved in the Cold War as an alternative to Soviet Union or US alliance. However, this rationale is contradictory as Beijing and Moscow also see themselves dominating their spheres of influence, geographically, economically and at times ideologically. In many developing states, particularly Africa, Beijing does buy influence with aid and a laissez-faire human rights criteria. However, China is also perceived by some as exploitative and exercising a competitive mercantilism that wipes away local competitors and reminds of previous European neocolonial powers.

China's appetite for natural resources is being gradually tempered by the maturing of its own export-based economy. As prices for commodities drop, the premiums enjoyed by those selling to China will shrink and potentially evolve toward more adversarial rather than compatible agendas. One has to also wonder if Beijing feels inclined to renegotiate its recent massive deal to purchase Russian natural gas and oil. In other words, the apparent glut, or at least one inflicted by Washington and allies, has disrupted not only prices but what were probably perceived as longer standing economic interests of mutual benefit.

Contagion risk or windfall opportunity?

In real combat, soldiers and civilians are killed, frequently all are targets. Economic warfare and sanctions though also have ordinary people as at least collateral casualties. Trying to temper the leadership in Moscow or Iran or … well, it certainly may be the only or at least better option than military conflict to counter the unbounded ambitions of despots as Putin. An additional bonus, we may be able to avoid World War 3. However, economic warfare can also be like mustard gas, if the wind blows back the wrong way. Sanctions on a smaller state may only marginally impact broader global economic health. However, globalisation has created the opportunity for both symbiosis and contagion. Whether the threat is real or not, it is no coincidence that the fate of European and US equity markets has also swung with the decline and/or rise of the Rouble, even if the Russian economy is dwarfed by that of the US, EU or China. Most notably, global investor sentiment and that of consumers may be swayed not so much by the tangible or the known but the uncertainty that darkens as 2015 dawns.

A drop in energy prices should be a huge windfall for most developed economies, a wind in their sails even as malaise has been the recent history. The resilience of the US economy gives optimism. Perhaps the medicine may finally heal ailing and East Asia economies. However, not all are winners or even survivors where disruption targeted and otherwise may claim unforeseen casualties of economic conflict and cloud the confidence of investors and consumers more broadly.

⇨   The above information is reprinted with kind permission from *Huffington Post*. Please visit www. huffingtonpost.com for further information.

Nuclear war: how scared should we be?

John Humphreys

The tense stand-off between North Korea and the United States, and the increasingly provocative rhetoric used by the leaders of each country against the other, have made the risk of nuclear weapons actually being used seem greater than at any time in recent history.

A false move by either could precipitate it and the consequences, all agree, would be catastrophic. But we have lived with the nuclear threat for 70 years and to a large extent have accustomed ourselves to it as just another fact of life. Have we become too complacent? How scared should we be?

The conflict between North Korea and the US seems more dangerous than any other recent conflict because of the extent to which both sides seem utterly determined to have their way. North Korea boasts of its ability to become a nuclear-armed state and is relentlessly pursuing its goal. Recent missile tests have extended the possible range of any nuclear weapons it might build so that the west coast of America might soon be a viable target. In the last week intelligence reports have suggested the country may be much further advanced than previously thought in being able to miniaturise a nuclear warhead so that it could be carried on such long-range missiles. The threat to the US looks increasingly close.

At the same time President Trump has made it abundantly clear that the United States will not tolerate North Korea achieving such power. Mr Trump said last week that he would rain down fire and fury such as the world had never seen if North Korea went too far. Kim Jong-un, the young North Korean leader, responded by threatening to test a (non-nuclear) missile just off America's Pacific island of Guam. Mr Trump retaliated by musing that his first threat had perhaps been too moderate.

What especially alarms even those observers used to confrontations between countries are the personalities of the two leaders facing up to each other. Some regard Kim Jong-un as a madman who would sooner see his country fry than abandon his ambition. Others, who dismiss the 'madman' label and regard him as being as rational as any other leader, are no less alarmed. They believe he is pursuing a logic that is far from irrational: that becoming a nuclear power is the only sure way he can see to entrench his regime in power. He has watched what happened to Saddam Hussein and Colonel Gaddafi when they lacked nuclear weapons to deter attack and he doesn't want to go the same way.

As for the hope of Donald Trump proving to be steady in a crisis, some are equally concerned. In the view of some experts who have studied his psychology and behaviour, the American president suffers from a narcissistic personality disorder in which he sees himself as a permanent victim who lashes out with uncontrollable anger when he feels he has been snubbed. Being provoked by Kim Jong-un may ultimately prove intolerable to him and he is the man – the only man – with his finger on the button of America's nuclear arsenal. No-one can stop him pushing it.

To some, however, any prediction of a potential Armaggedon is much too overblown. They point out that Donald Trump is surrounded by 'grown-ups', highly experienced military figures intent on preventing Armageddon. While not resiling from the determination of the President (and his predecessors) to stop North Korea in its tracks, these figures have publicly deployed the carrot as well as the stick, saying the United States is still ready to resume negotiations. Mr Trump has said so himself.

Some point to the Iran deal, brokered by Barack Obama, as the way forward. Long and patient diplomacy ended in an agreement in which Iran's ability to develop nuclear weapons was at the very least put on pause if not halted altogether. But there is a big difference. The Iranians always claimed not to want nuclear weapons. Even if many didn't (and still don't) believe them, their stance made possible a deal in which that particular can has been effectively kicked down the road. North Korea, however, makes no bones about its intentions and their logic is clear. So even with Russia and China onside, it is hard to see what diplomatic deal could be struck that could satisfy all sides.

In the face of this potentially hugely dangerous stand-off, there is, however, a completely different response, albeit one not advocated by anyone in power in the United States. It's to let North Korea have its nuclear weapons in order to make the world safer.

The case behind this apparently contrarian view is that deterrence works. That, say its proponents, is the lesson of the nuclear stand-off of 40 years between the United States and the Soviet Union. A confrontation between ideologies and national interests was converted from something with the potential to produce hot wars into a cold war by the fact that both sides had nuclear arms.

Another example of the supposed effectiveness of nuclear deterrence is the story of the antagonism between India and Pakistan, who gained independence from Britain 70 years ago this week. Conventional wars were fought regularly between the two until both got nuclear weapons; since then, there have been only skirmishes, not war.

The logic of this approach would seem to be that the way to make the world safer is for every country that wants to become a nuclear power to be allowed to do so. Yet even convinced believers in deterrence theory have baulked at this. At the same time as existing nuclear powers (including Britain) were building up their nuclear arsenals, they were devising means to prevent others from joining the nuclear club. They negotiated the Non-Proliferation Treaty in which, in return for abjuring the ambition to have nuclear weapons, countries outside the club were assisted in developing nuclear energy policies. That the latter would not lead to the former was dealt with through a stringent inspection regime.

In short, those who held a belief in nuclear deterrence, adopted a parallel (possibly contradictory) belief in "the fewer nuclear states, the better". Their reason lay in the possibility of accidents and in the danger of nuclear weapons falling into the hands of maverick leaders. This, after all, is why George W Bush and Tony Blair claimed they had to go to war against Saddam Hussein.

So we live in a world that both believes and doesn't believe in nuclear deterrence. Meanwhile history carries on producing wars such as those now being waged in Syria, Yemen and elsewhere, which we on the outside earnestly regret and do what we can to bring to an end, but which do not affect us directly. We assume that the future will continue to throw them up. The question is, though, whether deterrence theory has persuaded us that the casualties of such wars will continue to be measured in the thousands, maybe hundreds of thousands, but that war will never escalate into a nuclear exchange that would claim the lives of millions.

Those of us old enough to remember the Cuban Missile Crisis of 1962 recall the intense public fear of that long weekend. Many people believed it could well be the last weekend that they would see before being fried. It is hard to detect even the shadow of such fear now, even as the confrontation between North Korea and the United States presents the world with perhaps the greatest risk it has seen since then.

Have we become complacent about the nuclear threat? Should we be more scared? Or should we not be too bothered what Kim Jong-un and Donald Trump might get up to?

14 August 2017

⇨ The above information is reprinted with kind permission from YouGov. Please visit www.yougov.co.uk for further information.

Nukes, gaps, and international law – clearing metaphorical entanglements

Nobuo Hayashi

Some 20 years ago next week, on 8 July 1996, the International Court of Justice (ICJ) issued an advisory opinion regarding nuclear weapons. In a decision that split its 14-member bench, the court found, with the president's casting vote:

"The threat or use of nuclear weapons would generally be contrary to the rules of international law applicable in armed conflict, and in particular the principles and rules of humanitarian law; however, in view of the current state of international law, and of the elements of fact at its disposal, the Court cannot conclude definitively whether the threat or use of nuclear weapons would be lawful or unlawful in an extreme circumstance of self-defence, in which the very survival of a State would be at stake"

This ruling has given rise to divergent positions about the lawfulness of nuclear weapons. Some stand by the notion that there is no room left for their lawful use. On this view, the only thing that is perhaps missing is a treaty confirming their illegality. For many others, including myself, international law currently lacks a clear-cut, comprehensive prohibition against their use. This absence is paradoxical, since biological and chemical weapons, the other two weapons of mass destruction, are categorically banned regardless of the circumstances of their use. Still others interpret the advisory opinion as rightly conceding that today's international law permits the use of nuclear weapons in exceptional circumstances.

There is a legal gap

In December 2014, the Vienna conference on the humanitarian impact of nuclear weapons concluded with Austria's observation that "there is no comprehensive legal norm universally prohibiting [their] possession, transfer, production and use". The 'Austrian Pledge' – which is also a UN General Assembly resolution now and enjoys the official endorsement of more than 120 states – calls upon states "to identify and pursue effective measures to fill the legal gap for the prohibition and elimination of nuclear weapons".

The 'gap' metaphor quickly caught on. In April 2015, two international NGOs active in the field jointly published *Filling the Legal Gap: The Prohibition of Nuclear Weapons*. They argued that negotiations should commence in 2015 with a view to concluding a ban treaty. When that year's review conference of the Non-Proliferation Treaty (NPT) ended without a final document, a sizeable group of states decried a "reality gap, a credibility gap, a confidence gap and a moral gap" in what nuclear disarmament should mean. Those for whom customary international law already prohibits nuclear weapons insist that there is no legal gap but only a "compliance gap" with their prohibition.

There is no legal gap

Resistance to the metaphor has also become increasingly vocal. Let us focus on one of the two senses, i.e. the prohibition of nuclear weapons, in which the existence of a legal gap is contested. (The other sense concerns the content of disarmament obligations under the NPT's Article VI. The United States challenges the notion that there is any legal gap there. So does Italy.)

In April this year, Canada and The Netherlands filed papers with a UN open-ended working group where many participants echoed the need to fill the prohibition gap. The Dutch paper does not specifically deny the "so-called" legal gap. Instead, it quotes the ICJ's 1986 Nicaragua judgement that found that general international law imposes no limitation on the level of armaments of a state. The paper also highlights the 1996 advisory opinion's ambivalence. All we get is the impression that The Netherlands sees no legal gap insofar as "international law does not contain

any rule prohibiting nuclear weapons as such".

Canada's position – which it reiterated during the working group meetings – is more explicit. For Canada, "[t]he mere fact that a law or legal norm has not been imposed does not necessarily mean there is a legal gap". While seeking a ban "is an understandable aspiration, the reality is that under current customary international law, the use and possession of nuclear weapons is not illegal". Canada cautions that "legal gap arguments have the potential to be wrongly interpreted as implying there are legal grounds, as opposed to moral or humanitarian grounds, to negotiate a ban on nuclear weapons".

In Canada's view, "a true legal gap requires a situation where the absence of a law or legal norm prevents an inherently 'illegal' situation from being addressed". A New Zealand diplomat succinctly rebutted this mysterious notion called "inherent illegality". Nevertheless, Canada could be implying that a gap exists only where positive law fails to codify what is already forbidden. Since today's customary international law does not ban nuclear weapons per se, the absence of a ban treaty is not a legal gap.

Legal gap or no legal gap – that is not the question

The 'no legal gap' argument suggests that the absence of a prohibition does not necessarily mean the absence of a rule. By declining to ban nuclear weapons in all circumstances, international law implicitly permits their use in some circumstances. Permission is a rule, even if it is an implicit one.

This, to be sure, is all very engrossing stuff for lawyers. Delightfully esoteric and full of technical nuances, this line of reasoning raises the kinds of questions on which doctoral dissertations are written and legal careers built. Does today's international law still permit by default what it does not specifically prohibit? Is state survival really a right under international law? Did the ICJ effectively declare *non liquet* ("the law is not clear") in 1996 and, if so, did

it have the authority to do so? The list goes on.

The whole 'is there or is there not a legal gap' debate is a bit of a digression, however. For those who see a gap in nuclear weapons' international law status, the gap refers to the absence of their prohibition, not the absence of a rule on their use. Most of us involved in this discussion agree that the law presently lacks a nuclear weapons ban, whether we call it a legal gap or not.

Why, then, would anyone want to mask this agreement? This, I suspect, is because the deniers of a 'legal gap' are trying to denigrate the real preoccupation of their opponents. On the one hand, as long as the law contains no gap, there is, by definition, no gap to fill. The world can go back to the usual business of nuclear disarmament in good conscience. On the other hand, admitting a gap's existence would in practice mean admitting the need to fill it. If we successfully prevented the absence of a prohibition of nuclear weapons from being portrayed as a legal gap, that should undercut the ban advocacy's validity.

Advocating a nuclear weapons ban treaty is not an abstract exercise done for some aesthetic reasons ('a gap must be filled because it is there'). Rather, 'filling the legal gap' is a figure of speech that helps visualise the lack of a categorical prohibition of nuclear weapons as a problem in need of a solution. The metaphor also highlights prohibition as an item conspicuously missing in the catalogue of effective nuclear disarmament measures

proposed by nuclear-armed and umbrella states.

Let us call a spade a spade

In his declaration appended to the ICJ's 1996 advisory opinion, President Bedjaoui warned against those "who will inevitably interpret [the controversial paragraph] as contemplating the possibility of States using nuclear weapons in exceptional circumstances". He continued: "I feel obliged in all honesty to construe that paragraph differently, a fact which has enabled me to support the text."

For those who see a legal gap, filling it simply means introducing a general nuclear weapons ban. For those who do not, international law permits nuclear weapons in some situations. More importantly for them, this permission is in fact a nonissue. No need to fix the law, because it works fine as it is – this, ultimately, is what it means to say that there is no legal gap.

⇨ The above information is reprinted with kind permission from *Huffington Post*. Please visit www.huffingtonpost.com for further information.

North Korea panics the world, but 'H-bomb' test changes little

An article from The Conversation.

By Virginia Grzelczyk

North Korea has conducted its sixth nuclear device test, and based on what we know so far it looks like by far the biggest yet. Pyongyang's own news agency, KCNA, described the test as a "perfect success", and claimed the device was an advanced hydrogen bomb small enough to fit atop a long-range missile.

Though it's still too soon to confirm whether that's true, whatever the north tested was clearly much larger than its previous devices. Seismic readings detected the blast via a 6.3 magnitude earthquake, and Norway's NORSAR seismological observatory suggested the explosive yield would translate to a massive 120 kilotons.

After an extremely tense few months of tough rhetoric, missile launches, military exercises and troop movements, it seems North Korea has come very close to achieving what it's always said it was after: a viable missile-borne thermonuclear deterrent. So has the time finally come to run for the bomb shelters?

Before answering that, it pays to take stock of what the north has been up to of late – and why.

The best-laid plans

As of 4 September, North Korea had tested more than 20 missiles in 2017. Some were short-range, some medium-range; many of them were targeted to land into the East China Sea. Some launches failed, but one flew over northern Japan. None of these launches took place in a vacuum. They are part of a delicate, almost choreographed interplay between East Asia's most important actors, a dance of military moves, domestic political shuffling and international aspirations.

The Korean peninsula's problems always come down to the unresolved issues of Korean partition, the post-Korean War armistice, and the thousands of US troops permanently stationed in the region for the sake of Japan and South Korea's reconstruction and protection. The American military presence is a direct threat to the security of the Pygonyang power elite, and provides a pretext for the Kim government to claim it needs a massive military and a nuclear deterrent.

In the last year, the north has been especially concerned with the US's deployment of the the Terminal High Altitude Area Defence (THAAD) system, a Lockheed Martin-manufactured ballistic missile interceptor. THAAD is controversial in China and South Korea too, but it had arrived on the peninsula by March. By then, North Korea had already tested a new Pukguksong-2 missile, apparently assassinated Kim Jong-un's stepbrother, Kim Jong-nam, and launched four intermediate-range ballistic missiles into the East China Sea on 6 March.

With THAAD partially deployed and operational by early May, and with a new South Korean president assuming office, North Korea fired off various other missiles of other ranges in the ensuing weeks. The US, meanwhile, conducted its usual joint missile drills with South Korea and dispatched military ships to waters near the Korean peninsula.

The international community also condemned, as is customary, all of the launches with the standard volley of castigations: unacceptable, deplorable, beyond the pale. It all culminated on 5 August with United Nations Security Council Resolution 2371, which further targets North Korean exports and imports and its foreign workers.

Clearly that resolution hasn't deterred the north from its plans. But though this test looks like a giant step, technologically and politically speaking, it's only a small one.

Business as usual?

While the world's attention was mostly focused on the diplomatic tit-for-tat – and especially with what Donald Trump would do when forced to take an actual decision on North Korea – a number of sources, including the site 38 North, were already reporting that the established Punggye-ri test site was prime and ready for a new nuclear test, and had been as early as April. That in itself was hardly surprising; a bigger, more mobile bomb is just latest step in the nuclear programme, and has always been on the agenda.

Yet Pyongyang still hasn't made it all the way. Even if it might (and only might) be able to fit a hydrogen bomb onto a missile, it still has to solve other stubborn technical problems, particularly how to design long-range missiles that can re-enter the atmosphere without burning up.

Meanwhile, in the absence of ill-advised and highly unpredictable military action, the international community seems to have little up its sleeve other than sanctions and tough rhetoric. So far, both have failed – and they could be starting to backfire.

When Donald Trump threatened the north with "fire and fury" in retaliation for its long-range missile tests, I suggested it was likely that his inflammatory rhetoric would only spur Pyongyang to test yet more missiles. It seems this will continue. As soon as he woke up to the news of the latest nuclear test, Trump not only suggested that North Korea was a rogue nation, unsurprising, but that it was an embarrassment to China.

This is a fundamental misunderstanding. Yes, Chinese trade is vital to the North Korean economy, but Pyongyang is responsible for its own behaviour. This crisis draws its energy not from China's supposed enabling, but from the way North Korea understands its own security and protection – and as mentioned above, that worldview dates all the way back to the Korean armistice and its unresolved problems.

As things stand, it's clear that the north has developed enough technology to claim the title of 'nuclear power', and whether or not other nations think it has the right to be regarded as such is irrelevant. Equally, any military incursion on northern territory would very likely meet with retaliation from what's now a nuclear-armed state, meaning any discussion of conventional military intervention is effectively moot.

All the parties involved are fully aware of this. And as such the only way forward in this crisis is through some sort of dialogue about how to control the north's nuclear arsenal. When the safety of millions is at stake, talking with an opponent is no sign of weakness.

4 September 2017

⇨ The above information is reprinted with kind permission from *The Conversation*. Please visit www.theconversation.com for further information.

Ten lessons from North Korea's nuclear programme

By Richard N. Haass

North Korea has produced a number of nuclear warheads and is developing ballistic missiles capable of delivering them around the world. Many governments are debating how to prevent or slow further advances in North Korea's capacity and what should be done if such efforts fail.

These are obviously important questions, but they are not the only ones. It also is important to understand how North Korea has succeeded in advancing its nuclear and missile programmes as far as it has, despite decades of international efforts. It may be too late to affect North Korea's trajectory decisively; but it is not too late to learn from the experience. What follows are ten lessons that we ignore at our peril.

First, a government that possesses basic scientific know-how and modern manufacturing capability, and is determined to develop a number of rudimentary nuclear weapons, will most likely succeed, sooner or later. Much of the relevant information is widely available.

Second, help from the outside can be discouraged and limited but not shut down. Black markets exist anytime there is a profit to be made. Certain governments will facilitate such markets, despite their obligation not to do so.

Third, there are limits to what economic sanctions can be expected to accomplish. Although sanctions may increase the cost of producing nuclear weapons, history suggests that governments are willing to pay a significant price if they place a high enough value on having them. There is also evidence that some or all of the sanctions will eventually disappear, as other governments come to accept the reality of a country's nuclear status and choose to focus on other objectives. That is what happened in the case of India.

Fourth, governments are not always willing to put global considerations (in this case, opposition to nuclear proliferation) ahead of what they see as their immediate strategic interests. China opposes proliferation, but not as much as it wants to maintain a divided Korean peninsula and ensure that North Korea remains a stable buffer state on its borders. This limits any economic pressure China is prepared to place on North Korea over its nuclear efforts. The United States opposed Pakistan's development of nuclear weapons, but was slow to act, owing to its desire in the 1980s for Pakistani support in fighting the Soviet Union's occupation of Afghanistan.

Fifth, some three-quarters of a century since they were first and last used, and a quarter-century after the Cold War's end, nuclear weapons are judged to have value. This calculation is based on security more than prestige.

Decades ago, Israel made such a calculation in the face of Arab threats to eliminate the Jewish state. More recently, Ukraine, Libya and Iraq all gave up their nuclear weapons programmes either voluntarily or under pressure. Subsequently, Ukraine was invaded by Russia, Iraq by the US and Libya by the US and several of its European partners. Saddam Hussein in Iraq and Muammar el-Qaddafi in Libya were ousted.

North Korea has avoided such a fate, and the third generation of the Kim family rules with an iron fist. It is doubtful that the lesson is lost on Kim Jong-un.

Sixth, the Non-Proliferation Treaty–the 1970 accord that underpins global efforts to discourage the spread of nuclear weapons beyond the five countries (the US, Russia, China, the United Kingdom and France) that are recognised as legitimate nuclear weapons states for an unspecified but limited period of time–is inadequate. The NPT is a voluntary agreement. Countries are not obliged to sign it, and they may withdraw from it, with no penalty, if they change their minds. Inspections meant to confirm compliance are conducted largely on the basis of information provided by host governments, which have been known not to reveal all.

Seventh, new diplomatic efforts, like the recent ban on all nuclear weapons organised by the United Nations General Assembly, will have no discernible effect. Such pacts are the modern-day equivalent of the 1928 Kellogg-Briand Pact, which outlawed war.

Eighth, there is a major gap in the international system. There is a clear norm against the spread of nuclear weapons, but there is no consensus or treaty on what, if anything, is to be done once a country develops or acquires nuclear weapons. The legally and diplomatically controversial options of preventive strikes (against a gathering threat) and preemptive strikes (against an imminent threat) make them easier to propose than to implement.

Ninth, the alternatives for dealing with nuclear proliferation do not improve with the passage of time. In the early 1990s, the US considered using military force to nip the North Korean programme in the bud, but held off for fear of triggering a second Korean War. That remains the case today, when any force used would need to be much larger in scope and uncertain to succeed.

Finally, not every problem can be solved. Some can only be managed. It is much too soon, for example, to conclude that Iran will not one day develop nuclear weapons. The 2015 accord delayed that risk, but by no means eliminated it. It remains to be seen what can be done vis-à-vis North Korea. Managing such challenges may not be satisfying, but often it is the most that can be hoped for.

27 July 2017

⇨ The above information is reprinted with kind permission from Project Syndicate. Please visit www.project-syndicate.org for further information.

New technology for land mine detection

I n Colombia, large areas are teeming with mines that are almost impossible to detect with traditional methods. In collaboration with partners from South America, engineers at the German Ruhr-Universität Bochum and Technical University Ilmenau are developing a new mine clearance technology, based on ground penetrating radar. In the long run, they are aiming at creating a handheld device that will detect different mine types on rough terrain without fail and which can be used in the same way as metal detectors. The Ruhr-Universität's science magazine *Rubin* has published a detailed reported on the project.

In Colombia, large areas are teeming with mines. Finding them using traditional technologies is as good as impossible, because all mines are different.

In collaboration with partners from South America, engineers at the Ruhr-Universität Bochum and Technical University Ilmenau are developing an advanced method for humanitarian mine clearance in Colombia, which is based on ground penetrating radar technology. In the long run, they are aiming at developing a handheld device that will detect different mine types on rough terrain without fail.

Land mines almost impossible to detect with traditional methods

Even though Colombia has not experienced any military conflicts, many areas are teeming with land mines which had been laid by guerrilla forces and members of drug cartels. Because the booby traps were not industrially manufactured but had been assembled from various everyday objects, they are almost impossible to detect with traditional methods.

In the first step, the international research team built a number of land mines from everyday items, with empty detonators instead of explosives. They were used as templates for virtual computer models, which the engineers used to simulate the radar signal that each mine would generate.

Simulation of radar signals

The engineers analysed the simulated radar signals to identify properties that are typical for mines, but are not generated by other objects, such as stones or shrapnel. This information is fed into the analysis of the gathered radar data; this is how they set up their system to perform an automated search for properties that are typical for mines.

In theory, the method works. Now, the engineers have to get it up and running in reality and optimise it for application in a handheld device. According to their estimates, it will take another two to three years for a prototype to be completed.

Mine clearance in Colombia agreed upon

In 2015, the FARC guerrilla and the Colombian Government agreed on a comprehensive mine clearance. To date, the country's military has been mainly using metal detectors to search for booby traps. However, the traps contain barely any metal, and there are many other metal objects in the ground.

"Only one in 2,000 found objects is a mine," says Dr Christoph Baer from the Institute of Electronic Circuits in Bochum, who collaborates with Jan Barowski and Jochen Jebramcik from the Institute of Microwave Systems at the Ruhr-Universität. This renders the search extremely difficult.

Baer: "All mines must be found, because it is a humanitarian project." This is why the team knows that they won't file any patents. The technology they develop is meant to be publicly available.

18 March 2016

⇨ The above information is reprinted with kind permission from *Science Daily*. Please visit www.sciencedaily.com for further information.

View on disability: inventive ways to clear landmines

By Aisling Irwin

Since 1975, landmines have killed or maimed more than a million people, 80 per cent of them civilians. The disabilities caused by mines are devastating. And, in countries where access to physiotherapy and prostheses is poor – that is, most countries where landmines exist – the lifelong impact on well-being is extreme.

Last week's Anti-Personnel Mine Ban Convention conference in Switzerland was a reminder that the signatories hope to have eliminated mines within nine years. In that time, more than 100 million mines must be cleared from over 57 countries – and more unexploded bombs are appearing in countries such as Syria and Yemen every day, despite international treaties banning them.

Yet, while scientists regularly invent new ways of detecting mines, their relationship with mine clearance communities is often poor. This is partly because well-meaning inventors often bombard clearance organisations with wacky ideas that don't appreciate the complex realities of their work.

To find out what can be done, I rang Yann Yvinec, of the Royal Military Academy in Belgium. He has just finished coordinating TIRAMISU, a multimillion dollar project designed to bring scientists and mine clearers together to solve problems identified by the clearance community itself, rather than what scientists think they need.

Yvinec says the key was to bring onboard those involved in demining right from the start. The 26 research institutions and engineering companies involved in the programme were guided not just by a scientific board but also an 'end-user board' – those who will use the technologies – at every stage of the project.

They also brought in a technology marketing company to help analyse why deminers might not use new designs. This assessment and conversations with mine clearers highlighted the need for technology to be simple to use, robust – and cheap.

Through this early interaction, scientists realised several further truths. First, says Yvinec, deminers regularly risk their lives, so caution and infallible tools are far more important to them than speed or flashy gadgetry.

Second, a human inching along with a metal detector is, though slow, very accurate. "Metal detectors work very well now. There's little you can do to improve them," Yvinec says. "Improving detection itself is not where you can achieve the most in demining."

Instead, the area crying out for more and better solutions is all the work you have to do up to the point of removing landmines – the less glamorous and inefficient work at the beginning to narrow down the target area, before the clearers go in, for example. "The clearers can spend days and days and weeks without finding a single mine," he says.

The toolbox of innovations that TIRAMISU came up with includes techniques for distinguishing which suspected areas are actually mined.

These include a remote control aerial drone, equipped with sensors, which can gather data above suspected minefields. There is a tablet device that can digitise and organise the many types of information surveyors gather about an area – from villagers' testimonies and military maps, to the opinions of military strategists and topographical information.

A device under development tests the air above a suspected minefield for the scent of explosives. And there is an armoured tractor – cheaper, smaller, lighter and more manoeuvrable than its tank-like predecessors – for clearing vegetation and performing other tasks for demining teams.

TIRAMISU has now finished, but mine clearance organisations have already begun buying the new technologies. And the conversations haven't stopped. "We are trying to build a centre of excellence, a community to keep the link between all of us and the mine action communities," says Yvinec.

10 March 2016

⇨ The above information is reprinted with kind permission from SciDev Net. Please visit www.scidev.net for further information.

Belfast to be at forefront of UK nuclear deterrent with new warship

Belfast will be at the forefront at the forefront of the UK's nuclear deterrent.

By Jonathan Bell

Defence Secretary Michael Fallon has unveiled the name of one of the Navy's new warships will be called HMS *Belfast*.

The new Type 26 frigate is one of eight of the new City Class of frigates.

HMS *Belfast* will provide advanced protection for the likes of the UK's nuclear deterrent and Queen Elizabeth Class aircraft carriers. The Defence Secretary revealed the name at Belfast shipyard Harland and Wolff, which built the Royal Navy's last HMS Belfast, in 1939. It is now permanently moored in the Thames in London and operated by the Imperial War Museum. It will be renamed ahead of the maiden voyage of the new ship.

The new HMS *Belfast* is set to enter service in the mid-2020s and, along with her fellow Type 26 frigates, will have a truly global reach, protecting the UK's strategic interests as well as the likes of the UK's nuclear submarines, and delivering high-end warfighting capability wherever it is needed.

Its flexible design will also enable these capabilities to be adapted to counter future threats, whilst the ships will also benefit from the latest advances in digital technology.

Part of the MOD's £178 billion equipment plan, the three ships being built under the first contract will safeguard 4,000 jobs in Scotland and across the UK supply chain until 2035. The Defence Secretary cut steel on HMS *Glasgow*, the first Type 26

Defence Secretary Sir Michael Fallon said: "I'm hugely proud that the second name announced of our eight cutting-edge new Type 26 frigates will be HMS *Belfast*. She and her sister ships

will form the backbone of our Navy well into the 2060s, keeping us safe by protecting the country's nuclear deterrent and new aircraft carriers.

"It's apt to name this ship at the famous site which built the very first HMS *Belfast*. Thanks to our ambitious new National Shipbuilding Strategy, this shipyard once again has the chance to be involved in building a British warship thanks to the competition to build a new class of light frigates for our growing Royal Navy."

The Defence Secretary launched the ambitious National Shipbuilding Strategy earlier in the month, and as part of that laid out plans for a first batch of another new class of frigates – the Type 31e.

A procurement process for those ships could see them shared between yards and assembled at a central hub. The warships will be built in the UK, with a price cap of no more than £250 million, and will be designed to meet the needs of both the Royal Navy and the export market.

The Defence Secretary has personally committed to visiting all of the UK's major shipyards in the run-up to industry bringing forward its solutions for the Type 31e class, as he looks to grow the Royal Navy fleet for the first time since World War Two.

Just before the start of the Second World War, the original HMS *Belfast* was commissioned, having been built at Harland and Wolff shipyard. She went on to support the Battle of North Cape, the Normandy landings and the Korean War.

The original ship now belongs to the Imperial War Museum and is permanently docked in London. Before

the new HMS *Belfast* commissions, the original HMS *Belfast* will be renamed HMS *Belfast* 1938, the year the ship was launched.

Admiral Sir Philip Jones, First Sea Lord and Chief of Naval Staff, said: "The City class theme has been chosen for the Type 26 frigates in order to reaffirm the bond between the Nation and it's Navy. We want to honour some of the great centres of industry and commerce in all parts of the United Kingdom, and few cities have such a rich maritime heritage as Belfast.

"The previous HMS *Belfast* (1938) is one of the most famous ships of the twentieth century, serving at the Battle of North Cape, in the Arctic campaign and at the Normandy landings, and later with the United Nations forces sent to Korea. It is wonderful that she survives today as a museum, but the Royal Navy believes that such a distinguished fighting name deserves to take its place once more in our operational fleet.

"A world leader in anti-submarine warfare, the new HMS *Belfast* will work with our allies in NATO and around the world to preserve the freedom and security that her predecessor fought so hard to secure."

27 September 2017

⇨ The above information is reprinted with kind permission from *The Belfast Telegraph*. Please visit www.belfasttelegraph.co.uk for further information.

War and democracy – who decides?

***An article from* The Conversation.**

THE CONVERSATION

By John Keane, Professor of Politics, University of Sydney

In March 2003, the Howard government involved Australia in an illegal military invasion of Iraq. The consequences of that war continue to be devastating for the people of Iraq and the wider Middle East. The prime minister was able to opt for invasion because in Australia the sovereign power to take the gravest decision, the commitment of the Australian Defence Force to international armed conflict, rests with the executive – in practice, often the PM alone – rather than with parliament.

Since 2014, further military deployments have taken place in Iraq. The bombing of Syria continues. Several months ago, the prime minister announced unqualified support in principle for the United States in possible military action against North Korea.

All these developments reinforce the dangers typically associated with secretive small-group decision-making. Closed decision-making breeds hubris; and hubris, the friend of folly and recklessness, often results in disasters. All are a curse for democracy. That is why the Sydney Democracy Network, in partnership with Australians for War Powers Reform, convened a public forum on the subject of the urgent need for war powers reform.

Held on the International Day of Peace, 21 September, War and Democracy – Who Decides? featured contributions from Paul Barratt AO, president of Australians for War Powers Reform and former secretary of the Department of Defence; Professor Gillian Triggs, former president of the Australian Human Rights Commission and lawyer and activist Kellie Tranter, whose edited contribution follows.

"When governments kill in large numbers they always do so for a good reason. We must be on guard against that"

Howard Zinn

Australian politicians talk about ending terrorism but they make decisions that carelessly or inadvertently stir the pot and radicalise people. This then reinforces the dominant public narrative and makes military incursions superficially acceptable. Unfortunately, vigorous debate in Australia is encouraged only within the limits imposed by "unstated doctrinal orthodoxy", particularly in relation to foreign policy.

Not only are the people who control what we know determining our future, the government secrecy surrounding Australia's historical record deliberately obfuscates our understanding of what is going on right now. Symptomatic is the way the Australian Defence Force (ADF) has recently been found to be one of the least transparent military coalition members in Syria. The ADF won't reveal "where they bomb, when they bomb or what they bomb".

Syria's recent history reads like a contemporary illustration of Chris Clark's conclusion in *Sleepwalkers: how Europe Went to War in 1914*. The Period analysed in the book shows that great powers had more than one enemy, and that executive decision-making was chaotic.

War was a consequence of decisions made in many places, with their effect being cumulative and interactive. These decisions were made by a gallery of actors who otherwise shared a fundamentally similar political culture.

On 9 September 2015, Australia's permanent representative to the United Nations, Gillian Bird, wrote to the UN Security Council president claiming that Article 51 of the UN Charter recognises the inherent right of states to act in individual or collective self-defence when an armed attack occurs against a UN member state. States must be able to act in self-defence when the government of the state where the threat is located is unwilling or unable to prevent attacks originating from its territory. Bird alleged that the Syrian Government had, by its failure to constrain attacks upon Iraqi territory originating from ISIS bases within Syria, demonstrated that it was unwilling or unable to prevent those attacks.

Unauthorised and uninvited

The Australian Government was not questioned about how Syria was unwilling or unable to prevent those attacks. It was not asked how airstrikes would affect the Syrian population and infrastructure.

There was no link between ISIS, a non-state actor, and Syria. ISIS was not acting under instructions from, or the direction or control of, the Syrian Government. Western governments made no attempt to work with the morally disgraceful Assad regime to actually enable it to prevent attacks emanating from its territory (and indeed Australia didn't recognise the legitimacy of the regime).

Moreover, the Syrian Government didn't invite us to carry out airstrikes in Syria, and there was no UN Security Council resolution authorising the use of force. Neither the Australian Government nor the opposition provided a clear explanation about why in August 2015 there was no clear legal basis for Australian involvement in Syria, but by September 2015 there was.

There was no rational discussion about our strategic ends. There was certainly no mention of the fact that in 2014 we already had embedded ADF personnel in Florida contributing to operations against ISIS in Syria.

There was, however, a letter, dated 17 September 2015, from the Syrian Government to the Security Council. The mainstream media did not report it, but the letter was referred to in documents I received following FOI requests. The letter disputed Australia's unwilling and unable claims and pointed out that the Syrian Arab Army had, over four years, been fighting ISIS, the al-Nusrah Front and other groups being supported by Turkey, Jordan, Saudi Arabia, Qatar and Western states.

The letter called on others to co-ordinate with Syria. It said the international coalition led by the US had yet to achieve anything tangible in its war on terrorist organisations.

The Syrian Government had a point, particularly since US President Barack Obama had already told *VICE News* (on camera) that:

ISIS is a direct outgrowth of al-Qaeda in Iraq that grew out of our invasion in 2003, which is an example of unintended consequences.

Failing Syria

What was omitted from the political and public discourse in the lead-up to Australia's decision to become involved in Syria was the fact that Syria had experienced a severe drought between 2007 and 2010. The drought spurred as many as 1.5 million people to migrate from the countryside into the cities, creating significant social and economic tensions.

In 2012 the UK's MI6 co-operated with the CIA on a 'rat line' of arms transfers from Libyan stockpiles to Syrian rebels after the fall of the Gaddafi regime. That same year, Russia proposed that Assad could step down as part of a peace deal. The US, Britain and France were so convinced that the Syrian dictator would fall that they ignored the proposal.

By this stage, the UN human rights commissioner had already confirmed 60,000 Syrian fatalities between March 2011 and November 2012. The current estimate is almost half a million deaths.

In September 2014 the US Congress determined that the US$500 million CIA program to arm Syrian rebels had failed. Arms had been ending up in the hands of the al-Nusra Front, and Jordanian intelligence officers were selling arms on the black market.

The following month, The New York Times reported that a CIA report had concluded that "many past attempts by the agency to arm foreign forces covertly had a minimal impact on the long-term outcome of a conflict". The report came a month after Australia had delivered weapons to Kurdish Peshmerga fighters and a month before our successful delivery of 18,000kg of crated weapons from Albania to Erbil in Iraq.

On 21 March 2015, international aid agencies and human rights groups released the Failing Syria report. This found that UN Security Council powers had failed to alleviate the suffering of civilians as the conflict intensified.

Two months later, the International Crisis Group released its own report warning that military aid had been given without an underlying strategy, which would prolong the battle with ISIS and inflame other local conflicts between intra-Kurdish rivals. The report noted that the US-led coalition

had remained silent about Kurdish land grabs in disputed territories.

In May this year, Amnesty International urged the US and other countries to stop arms transfers that could fuel atrocities. This followed confirmation by a US Defence Department audit that the army had failed to monitor over US$1 billion worth of arms and other military equipment transfers to Kuwait and Iraq, which have ended up in the hands of ISIS.

A show for the domestic audience

In August 2015 rumours began to circulate that the then prime minister, Tony Abbott, had pushed for the US request to join airstrikes in Syria. Only five days before the bipartisan decision was made, Amnesty International reported that 220,000 people had been killed in Syria. Another 12.8 million needed humanitarian assistance and 50% of the population was displaced.

Still, at a reported cost of A$500 million a year for our air war against ISIS, and regardless of international law, we were first in with the US, beating our British counterparts who delayed plans for a parliamentary vote. A number of military strategists were of the view that Australia's involvement was a show for the domestic audience.

The irony, of course, is that six days after the decision to conduct airstrikes in Syria, we had a new prime minister. Shortly after that a document titled *ADF Operations in the Middle East* was produced in response to my FOI request. It confirmed that "the prospects for a political or military solution are poor".

The word 'poor' seems highly inadequate. In order to supply arms to Syrian rebels, the Pentagon relies on an army of contractors from military giants to firms linked to organised crime. Saudi Arabia (a Western ally) and Qatar are providing clandestine financial and logistical support to ISIS, while Iran and Russia support Assad. Turkey is fighting the Kurds and the US-supported opposition groups, but is fighting with Russia against ISIS.

There are drone strikes and bombs being dropped by the US, Belgium, Jordan, The Netherlands, Bahrain, Saudi Arabia, United Kingdom, France, United Arab Emirates, Turkey, Israel, Denmark and Australia. There is disturbing evidence of the al-Nusra Front's access to sarin gas. And to top it off, a Bulgarian journalist recently uncovered Azerbaijan Silk Way Airlines offering diplomatic flights to private companies and arms manufacturers from the US, Balkans and Israel and the militaries of Saudi Arabia, United Arab Emirates and US Special Operations Command to ship weapons around the world, including to Syria, without regulation.

Hidden agendas lead to humanitarian disaster

Our politicians continue to support the US, an ally that has historically forsaken the exploration of peaceful means and diplomatic solutions in favour of force and aggression. Under the pretext of responding "with decency and with force" to humanitarian concerns and the responsibility to protect civilians, Australia extended airstrikes into Syria.

Decency? Every war is a war on children when armed conflicts kill and maim more children than soldiers. Perversely, more soldiers die from suicide and peacetime incidents than war.

And then there's the matter of secrecy. On 6 January 2017, I issued an FOI request to the Defence Department for copies of documents confirming or specifying the dates, locations and outcomes (numbers of military and civilian casualties) of airstrikes by Australian forces in Syria. On 20 January 2017, I received an email simply confirming that "the Department does not specifically collect authoritative (and therefore accurate) data on enemy and/or civilian casualties in either Iraq or Syria and certainly does not track such statistics".

For all the political protestations about concern for civilian lives, we are not even trying to count our victims. To date, we have only claimed responsibility for the deaths of Syrian soldiers in airstrikes in September 2016.

This year, as if Australia wasn't already an aircraft carrier for the US, the government decided to sell military equipment to Saudi Arabia. Overnight, Defence Industry Minister Christopher Pyne became a dedicated arms salesman, announcing that he wanted Australia to become a major arms exporter on a par with Britain, France and Germany, and to use exports to cement relationships with countries in volatile regions such as the Middle East.

Perpetual war has devastated the Middle East. Others rightly argue that a government that devotes the bulk of its budget to arms manufacturing implicitly makes a moral decision that militarism is more important than the creation of well-being for the population.

The difficulty is that Australians still aren't told the truth about why we became involved in Syria. Those decisions seem to have been made in furtherance of unstated international coalition agendas rather than on open and objective assessments of their merit. This state of affairs is made profoundly worse by the fact that the decision to go to war was an executive decision, not a decision made democratically after full and open parliamentary debate based on the best objective information available.

We are fighting a difficult battle for transparency in these disturbingly Orwellian times, but the battle can and should be waged for as long as we have the will and the means to do so. Our best weapons are an accurate historical and geopolitical perspective and truth.

When it comes to war, our government needs to be more transparent and to open up decision-making on whether to become involved. Politicians and military personnel must be accountable for the human consequences of what they perpetrate in our name. It is our collective responsibility to do what we can to hold them to account

16 November 2016

⇨ The above information is reprinted with kind permission from *The Conversation*. Please visit www.theconversation.com for further information.

Britain shouldn't sell arms to the Saudis, no matter what promises they make

An article from The Conversation.

By Riccardo Labianco

THE CONVERSATION

Since the catastrophic Yemeni civil war began in 2015, the British public has woken up to a serious problem: the use of UK-manufactured arms by Saudi Arabia. Various NGOs, campaigners and many MPs are increasingly worried about evidence that since the beginning of the conflict, Saudi Arabia has used UK-manufactured arms in ways that violate international law.

The British Government, however, seems content to continue selling weapons to the Saudis – and indeed has worked hard to justify doing so. Government representatives have repeatedly claimed that the UK enjoys a "privileged position" from which it can train the Saudi armed forces and pressure them to comply with the international law of armed conflict. The corollary is that if the UK gave that position up, someone more nefarious would inherit it.

As the UK foreign secretary, Boris Johnson, said in the House of Commons in October 2016:

We would be vacating a space that would rapidly be filled by other Western countries that would happily supply arms with nothing like the same compunctions, criteria or respect for humanitarian law. More importantly, we would, at a stroke, eliminate this country's positive ability to exercise our moderating diplomatic and political influence on a crisis in which there are massive UK interests at stake.

The Government routinely falls back on this argument; it made the same case recently when it faced a judicial review of its decision to continue exporting arms to the Saudis despite their violations of humanitarian law.

The rationale has so far stood up in British courts and in parliament. But it is nonetheless deeply flawed – and

it doesn't come close to justifying what the Government is still doing. Instead, the British Government's legal arguments seem highly selective.

The law regulates arms exports between states in two ways. Some provisions require the supplier state to assess how the recipient will use the arms before it transfers them; other provisions apply after the recipient has actually used the arms unlawfully. The point is that once arms are exported to another country, it is very difficult for the supplier to control who is using them and how. This is why there are legal norms applying to both the misuse of arms in the future and suppliers' part in past violations.

But it's not unusual for supplier states to focus solely on 'guaranteeing' that arms won't be misused while avoiding responsibility for unlawful use in the past. This is the case for the British-Saudi transfers, where the UK Government seems content to talk about the guarantees that come with future transfers – even though the Saudis and their allies have violated humanitarian law with British weapons before.

At face value

In short, as far as international law is concerned, the Saudis' assurances for the future do not justify the UK's arms sales. A promise to behave properly in the future cannot justify unlawful behaviour in the past – especially not if the supplier state held a 'privileged position' over the recipient when those violations were committed.

More than that, since arms have a long lifespan and are often stored and recycled for future conflicts, they have a nasty way of escaping the supplier's control, making promises to limit their use essentially immaterial. This is precisely what has happened

in Yemen, where the Saudi-led coalition has reportedly used British-manufactured cluster munitions.

Cluster munitions release or disperse explosive sub-munitions over a wide area, meaning they cannot be precisely targeted. Their imprecision means they can do substantial collateral damage during a conflict and they also leave unexploded ordnance scattered over wide areas where it can injure or kill civilians who find it after a conflict is over. Because of their excessive impact, they have been banned since 2010.

In 2016, the UK defence secretary, Michael Fallon, reported that the British-manufactured cluster munitions used in Yemen arrived to Saudi Arabia in the early 1980s, 30 years before the international ban. But this misses the point: the UK may not be producing, stockpiling and exporting cluster munitions any longer, but its past exports of these weapons are still in use, and there's very little that can be done about it.

In any case, the argument that a 'privileged position' from which to influence buyers' behaviour justifies the UK's arms sales makes no sense. After all, even if the UK could control the way Saudi Arabia uses exported arms, that would surely implicate it in everything the Saudis do with them.

10 August 2017

⇨ The above information is reprinted with kind permission from *The Conversation*. Please visit www.theconversation.com for further information.

Conflict and the British arms trade

Public views on our role in the arms trade.

By Maria Stonehouse

According to 70% of the British public, the UK Government should not be promoting the sales of British military equipment to foreign governments that have poor human rights records.

When it comes to non-democratic countries, the level of opposition is similar: 60% think that it is wrong for the UK Government to promote the sale of British military equipment to foreign countries that are not democracies, such as dictatorships, military regimes and unstable states.

It appears that our role in arms fairs is also highly contested. Two thirds (64%) think that the Government should not be involved in the organisation of arms fairs if countries with poor human rights records are attending. Two in five (43%) think that the UK Government should not be involved in organising arms fairs at all.

When asked about whether the UK arms industry should sell British military equipment to Saudi Arabia, 62% said it should not be. 62% also said no when asked the same question on Israel, and an even larger 71% were in opposition when asked the same question for Pakistan.

⇨ The above information is reprinted with kind permission from Opinium Research. Please visit opinium.co.uk for further information.

© 2018 Opinium Research

Does the UK need a 'War Powers Act'?

By Andrew Noakes

In the wake of Chilcot, questions have been raised about the democratic accountability of the process involved in taking this country to war.

In the middle of a stormy night on 4 August, 1964, a US Navy warship patrolling the coast of North Vietnam detected radar and sonar signals in the Gulf of Tonkin that suggested it was about to come under attack. The USS *Maddox* spent several hours feverishly manoeuvring over rough seas and firing shells into the darkness. In the morning no evidence could be found of the enemy, but policy-makers in Washington nonetheless decided it meant war.

President Johnson immediately sought and gained permission from the US Congress to use "all necessary measures" against North Vietnam, which resulted in almost a decade of conflict. But by 1973, Congress was not happy. Many of its members claimed that, despite the 'Gulf of Tonkin Resolution' they had passed, their permission for a wider war had never been sought. They passed the War Powers Act that year: a law designed to ensure the president had to seek Congress' explicit consent for any decision to go to war in the future.

Britain has no such law. Here, the prime minister alone has the authority to send troops to war using Royal Prerogative Powers that were originally handed to her office during the Glorious Revolution of 1688. But even though the Government poured cold water over the idea of a War Powers Act earlier this year, it's slowly starting to creep onto the agenda. After the Chilcot report was released in July, Labour leader Jeremy Corbyn stated that a US-style War Powers Act would help to prevent the UK from going to war on false pretences. He has also suggested that it could stop the Government from sending special forces into secret wars without public awareness or consent.

Crispin Blunt, who chairs parliament's Foreign Affairs Committee, has similarly criticised the lack of parliamentary authorisation for special forces when they're being sent on long-term combat missions. Meanwhile, the House of Lords is currently considering its own version of a War Powers Act, the Armed Forces Deployment Bill.

So why not pass a War Powers Act? It worked for America, didn't it?

Well, not quite. The War Powers Act has never actually been invoked, despite the US being involved in several wars since the 1970s. Every president has claimed it is unconstitutional. So the lesson from America is that relying on a War Powers Act to provide a bulwark against unwarranted military action could be complicated.

Not least in the UK, where the ludicrously undemocratic Royal Prerogative Powers have been tempered over time by laws and conventions. Since 2003, a convention has emerged that is supposed to ensure that parliament has the opportunity to debate any decision to go to war. That started with Tony Blair's decision to consult parliament on the Iraq War, making any attempt to link the need for a War Powers Act to Chilcot and Iraq a bit of a stretch of the historical imagination. The convention was also applied to the question of intervening in Libya in 2011, and most recently in Syria at the end of last year.

The convention might seem to obviate the need for a War Powers Act. But its charm is also its flaw – it can be interpreted in many different ways. A hawkish government trying to seek a war without public scrutiny might claim that covert or indirect military action, such as embedding UK troops in foreign armies or using drones, is not included in the convention. Indeed, in recent responses to one question from Caroline Lucas MP and another from David Anderson MP, the current government appears to exclude both of these from its interpretation of the convention. At the same time, the Ministry of Defence is increasingly placing such methods at the forefront of its military strategy.

But intervention sceptics and advocates for accountability can also push for their own interpretations. In 2013 David Cameron was forced by backbench MPs from across the political divide to promise that parliament would have a vote over any decision to send arms to Syrian rebels.

A War Powers Act muddies the water, because its value as a check on government depends on what its writers choose to include and exclude. Indeed, a War Powers Act that

definitively does not cover drones, arming rebels, or the actions of embedded UK troops in foreign armies is actually worse for government accountability than a more flexible convention that could be applied to these methods should MPs demand it.

A case in point is the current Armed Forces Deployment Bill in the House of Lords. The Bill is essentially a War Powers Act, and it has been introduced in the welcome spirit of increasing transparency and accountability. But the way its definitions are drafted risks creating exemptions for drones, arming rebels, and embedded troops, and it definitively excludes special forces. It also doesn't have provisions that would apply retrospective approval to cover non-combat missions that subsequently escalate. It's strange to think that the UK military mission to Helmand started as a supposedly peaceful reconstruction mission, but became one of the most lethal military campaigns in modern UK history. And yet the proposed Bill in the Lords would not have subjected the decision to deploy over 3,000 troops there in 2006 to a vote.

So any War Powers Act politicians may be considering needs to be

drafted right. It can't exempt certain forms of warfare or fail to anticipate mission escalation. This is especially important given that remote forms of warfare, including drones, special forces, training missions, and foreign embedded troops, are expected to become the most common avenue for military intervention in the future. Right now UK special forces are fighting Islamic State all over Syria, Iraq and Libya, while British drones conduct regular strikes against Islamic State. UK forces are also believed to be advising on Saudi military operations in Yemen. To exclude these methods of fighting would make any War Powers Act futile. Bottom line – if you're going to do a War Powers Act, you'd better do it right.

23 September 2016

⇨ The above information is reprinted with kind permission from Oxford Research Group. Please visit www.oxfordresearchgroup.org.uk for further information.

© 2018 Oxford Research Group

'Everywhere around us was war'

The space around Nejebar's home is immaculate. A rug has been laid across the table and Nejebar straightens it out as we take our place there. It's late in the afternoon and the noises of the camp have given way to a quiet calmness. It strikes me that Nejebar has taken control of her family's situation here. There's a strength and steadiness about her. Her husband, Noor, looks a little disorientated by the experience.

The family is from Herat in Afghanistan. They tell of a traumatic experience in their homeland, which led them to flee.

> **"The only reason we left is because of the war. When we were there, every moment we were just trying to protect our children. Everywhere around us was war. There were people around us who died. The situation was very bad. We didn't come here for no reason"**

"My husband was working for the government and the Taliban was announcing that they were going to kill anybody who worked for the government. That was the most frightening part. If you were a teacher, or anything like that, they were saying that they were going to kill you, or cut your hands, or cut your throat. One day, the Taliban came to the house of a member of our family. They brought him out and cut his eyes out and killed him. He worked for the government."

The family arrived in Greece seven months ago and have been in the camp in Agios Andreas for six months now. They are thankful that they are in a country that is safe, but are struggling to live in this way, in the unknown. "We took the decision that it is better to die here than to die there from war.

"It is very peaceful here and it is safe. We are waiting for the borders to open. We thought we would wait here about ten days, but it is taking so long. We want a peaceful life. We want our children to have an education, to go to school. The most important thing is for our children. Not to stay like this… to not be able to go to school."

After the interview, as we are chatting, Hinayat (Nejebar's eldest son) says he has a question for us. "Why,..." he asks, "...did so many countries come into Afghanistan to help, but did not stay and finish?"

He looks at us, expectant of a reply. "Because...", my colleague Joseph says, "'..we always think we can just go in quickly and then leave, and instead we make a mess."

'They took my children'

When Ruhia sits down to share her story, she does so clutching a red wallet. As she talks she sobs, grief stricken, and opens it, removing two small photographs of a boy and a girl.

They were her children, killed by the Taliban.

Ruhia lifts the hem of her dress to reveal scars across her feet: wounds suffered when they attempted to cut her down as she fled.

After finally managing to escape from Afghanistan, Ruhia and her one surviving son made the perilous journey to Europe in search of sanctuary. She nearly drowned in the attempt.

'They took my children, the Taliban, and they killed them at the border. And they cut my feet with a knife. When I came here in the sea I almost drowned in the water. The coastguards came and they saved us. If they had come a few minutes later we would have been dead. In the place I lived there was a lot of Taliban. Every day they were bringing people and cutting their heads off. Then they put a bomb in our house and they told us if we came back they would cut us into pieces.'

When sadness prevents her from speaking, her friend Rahima comes to comfort her: a consolation only possible between people who share the same extremity of pain. Like Ruhia, Rahima has also endured the loss of a child: her son was taken by the Taliban.

"When some new people come here to the camp I think they are Taliban, too, or that they are going to hurt us. My heart is beating. I don't have anybody to help me.

"I am just in God's hands."

A person's pain cannot be measured. Yet the hours I spent with Ruhia revealed a depth of pain and suffering that I have not before witnessed. It staggers me that the human heart can hold such pain, and survive.

"At night we sit together as women, we drink tea, we tell our stories, and we cry together"

⇨ The above information is reprinted with kind permission from Christian Aid Collective. Please visit www.christianaidcollective.org for further information

© 2018 Christian Aid Collective

The Azure payment card

An extract from The Humanitarian Cost of a Cashless System.

By Carnet, P., Blanchard, C., Ellis, J. (2014). The Azure Payment Card: The Humanitarian Cost of a Cashless System. ISBN: 978-0-900228-17-9. London: British Red Cross. (Online).

Available: http://www.redcross.org.uk/~/media/BritishRedCross/Documents/About%20us/Research%20reports%20by%20advocacy%20dept/The%20Azure%20payment%20card%20report.pdf

The British Red Cross has a long tradition of providing practical and emotional support to vulnerable refugees and asylum seekers across the UK, including those refused asylum. Section 4 support is given to refused asylum seekers who are destitute and have agreed to return to their country of origin, but cannot return immediately due to circumstances beyond their control. It can also be given on human rights grounds if these refused and destitute asylum seekers have further submissions under consideration.

People on section 4 support have no access to cash. The support consists of accommodation, on a no-choice basis, and £35.39 a week via the Azure payment card. The card is only accepted by a few retailers and can only buy food, essential toiletries, clothing and credit for mobile phones.

The card cannot be used for travel or for items such as alcohol and cigarettes.

Research objectives

⇨ To explore the effectiveness of the Azure card in providing support to refused asylum seekers, from the viewpoint of organisations that work with them.

⇨ To understand refused asylum seekers' lived experience of using the Azure card.

Conclusion

The Azure card and section 4 support does not allow refused asylum seekers to meet their basic needs and live with dignity. It creates unnecessary suffering for people who are already in desperate situations.

The Red Cross would like the cost difference between the Azure card system and the previous cash system to be assessed. This has not yet been possible, since current information about Azure card costs is protected by commercial agreement.

Recommendations

⇨ The Red Cross advocates that the Azure payment card should be abolished.

⇨ We call for one integrated form of support throughout the asylum seeking process – from the person who has just arrived in the UK to someone who has been refused asylum.

⇨ This support (excluding accommodation costs) must be in the form of cash, as with other benefits.

These policy recommendations require the withdrawal of section 4 (11) (b) article of the Immigration and Asylum Act 1999, which forbids a person on section 4 support being supplied money. In the interim, we are asking for practical steps to be taken by the different stakeholders involved, including the Home Office, Sodexo, authorised retailers and the Red Cross itself

Research methodology

⇨ A questionnaire was distributed UK-wide to 104 organisations working with people on section 4 support (including Red Cross refugee services).

⇨ In-depth interviews were conducted with 11 Azure card users.

Key findings

People on section 4 support struggle to meet their basic needs because of Azure card restrictions.

⇨ 85% of the organisations in our survey feel that their clients are left hungry because section 4 support is insufficient.

⇨ 81% report that authorised retailers offer poor value for money.

Azure card users have difficulty understanding the payment system.

⇨ 79% of our survey respondents agree that their clients have particular difficulty in understanding how the carry-over limit works.

Staff at authorised shops do not fully understand the Azure card system.

⇨ All but one of the Azure card users we spoke to have experienced difficulties when trying to pay with the card.

⇨ 72% of our survey respondents report clients having their card refused in the previous six months.

⇨ 70% say their clients have experienced poor treatment from shop staff.

Azure card users experience technical difficulties when using the card – which can lead to a break in financial support.

⇨ 85% of our survey respondents report that their clients' cards have not worked at some point during the last six months. This sometimes happens despite users having a credit balance on the card.

⇨ Contacting the customer service line does not appear to be helpful and Azure card users can be left without financial support for several days.

Getting to the supermarket and essential appointments – such as medical and legal appointments – is hugely problematic.

⇨ Survey respondents indicate that distance (88%) and illness (82%)

can make it difficult to get to a shop that accepts the Azure card.

⇨ They also report that clients have difficulty travelling to visit legal representatives (94%) and health workers (92%) due to a lack of money.

⇨ Most of the Azure card users we interviewed did not know they could apply for specific travel support to attend medical appointments.

People on section 4 support struggle to stay healthy – which can increase the costs for other services.

⇨ 92% of the organisations in our survey feel that their clients on section 4 support are unable to maintain good health.

⇨ The Azure card system has a real impact on users' mental health.

Azure card users feel embarrassed, anxious and trapped.

⇨ Our survey respondents acknowledged feelings of embarrassment (88%) and anxiety (89%) when using the card.

⇨ More than half of our interviewees feel trapped because they do not have access to cash.

⇨ Asking friends for help makes them feel like a "beggar" and "desperate".

⇨ The above information is reprinted with kind permission from The British Red Cross. Please visit www.redcross.org.uk for further information.

UK aid agencies call for an end to Myanmar violence

Action Against Hunger UK, ActionAid UK, Christian Aid, Save the Children UK and the International Rescue Committee UK have issued a joint statement calling for an end to violence in Myanmar and immediate access for humanitarian aid.

"Action Against Hunger UK, ActionAid UK, Christian Aid, Save the Children UK and the International Rescue Committee UK strongly condemn the attacks carried out on 25 August.

"We are deeply concerned by the spiraling violence that has followed across Myanmar's northern Rakhine State. We are also concerned about reports of extensive loss of life of civilians and the immense suffering that is producing the displacement of thousands of people from their homes and livelihoods.

""The Myanmar Government has a responsibility and obligation to protect all of the civilian population without distinction. Violence is not a long-term solution to the challenges faced by all populations in Rakhine State.

"As humanitarian actors, we remind all parties of their responsibility to exercise restraint, avoid the targeting of civilians and prevent the further escalation of conflict in the area. It is also crucial that Myanmar national and local authorities facilitate access for UN agencies and international, national and local NGOs able to provide aid and immediate relief to the civilian population affected by the ongoing military and police operations.

"We are particularly concerned about reports of the impact that the conflict and displacement is having on women and girls. The Bangladesh government and local authorities should continue to ensure the safe passage of people fleeing the violence and providing aid to refugees upon arrival.

"As UK-based INGOs we call on the British Government to press for an end to violence and to use its international influence to encourage the Government of Myanmar to fulfil its obligations regarding ensuring humanitarian access and the protection of all civilians.

"Further we call on the UK and other donors to urgently make funds available to respond to the needs of those who have been displaced, in particular the estimated 400,000 people who have crossed into Bangladesh."

14 September 2017

⇨ The above information is reprinted with kind permission from ActionAid UK. Please visit www.actionaid.org.uk.

Islamic State launches unprecedented wave of suicide bombers to try to defend Mosul

By Raf Sanchez, Middle East Correspondent and Gareth Brown, Mosul

The Islamic State (Isil) has launched an unprecedented wave of suicide bombers, some of whom are children, against advancing Iraqi forces as the jihadist group struggles to hold on to its city stronghold of Mosul.

More than a hundred suicide bombers have hurled themselves at Iraqi troops since the Mosul offensive began on 17 October, a rate of self-annihilation never before seen even by the extreme standards of Isil.

"The amount of people killing themselves is unprecedented. It's completely different from anything we've seen before," said Charlie Winter, a senior fellow at the ICSR think tank who tracks the use of suicide bombers.

On one particularly bloody day on the battlefield in Mosul there were 18 separate suicide attacks within 24 hours. Mr Winter said that was more attacks than the al-Nusra Front, al-Qaeda's affiliate in Syria, had carried out in 100 days.

Many of the 102 suicide attacks have been carried out using improvised armoured vehicles which are packed to the brim with explosives and then driven at high speed at oncoming enemies.

Iraqi troops showed *The Sunday Telegraph* a Jeep that Isil engineers had covered entirely with armour plating, leaving only a small square of the windscreen open so that the suicide bomber driver could see his target. The vehicle was captured in the Christian village of Karemlesh before it could be put to use.

General Fadel Al-Barawi, a special forces commander, said that the jihadists were using suicide bombers in such large numbers because many of their best troops – especially foreign fighters from Chechnya – had already been killed or fled. "The only weapons they have now are suicide bombers and snipers, they are too reliant on these," he said.

At least two children are known to have killed themselves in suicide attacks in Mosul but the real figure is probably higher.

While Isil usually puts out detailed 'martyrdom notices' about its suicide bombers, Mr Winter found that in Mosul only a small number of the attackers have received these eulogies.

It may be that Isil's media arm was struggling to keep up with the number of attacks but could also be that the group was reluctant to show how many children it was using as suicide bombers, he said.

The Iraqi military released an extraordinary video on Saturday which showed soldiers pleading with a young jihadist not to blow himself up.

"My brother, you are too young," one soldier said as the youth stood in a suicide vest. "Let the leaders kill themselves, why have they asked you to blow yourself up? Don't do it, we are coming to save you."

It was not clear from the video if they succeeded in talking the would-be bomber out of carrying out his mission.

Among the wave of suicide bombers was an Irish jihadist named Terence Kelly, who styled himself as Abu Osama Irelandi after joining Isil in the so-called caliphate. The Dubliner blew himself up on Friday after driving a vehicle at a Shia militia group as it advanced into a village outside Mosul.

His death brought a violent end to the Irish nurse's long and troubled journey through radical Islam, which began in the 1990s when he converted in a Saudi prison after being arrested for illegally making alcohol.

Kelly, who was in his late 40s, became a prominent Islamist in Britain and a friend of the jailed hate preacher Anjem Choudary before eventually killing himself on the battlefields of Iraq.

Many of the bombs and the armoured vehicles are being manufactured in al-Karamah, an industrial district of Mosul where factories have been converted into bomb-making workshops. Iraqi special forces have entered the area but are encountering stiff resistance.

5 November 2016

⇨ The above information is reprinted with kind permission from *The Telegraph*. Please visit www.telegraph.co.uk for further information.

Iraq: the plight of the forgotten people

By Laura Taylor, Head of Advocacy, Christian Aid

The IDP crisis as it now stands is the result not only of ISIS's taking control of areas of Iraq (now ended of course) but also a result of the anti-ISIS coalition's operations to take back these areas from ISIS control.

In 2016 there were over three million people in Iraq who had been forced to flee their homes due to the violence and destruction caused by Isis and other internal sectarian conflicts.

The country is also hosting some 250,000 of the millions of refugees who have fled the war in Syria. Most are living in tiny Portakabins in vast camps, or are scraping together enough money to rent a very basic home in an unfamiliar place, where finding work, schooling or medical care is incredibly difficult.

I had the privilege of travelling to Iraqi Kurdistan in March 2016 to meet a tiny fraction of these people, to sit on the floor with them and hear their stories.

I met Amina, who escaped from Aleppo in Syria after Isis beheaded her brother and her husband went missing. She came to Iraq with her younger sisters, four-year-old son, elderly parents and ten-year-old nephew. Amina's mother needs a wheelchair and her father has struggled to find work, so her teenage sisters do long hours in a cake factory – their dreams of getting an education long-forgotten. Meanwhile Amina, supported by Christian Aid's local partner REACH, has trained to be a hairdresser.

Between them they earn just enough to rent a three-room unfinished house, with holes in the windows and walls. Here, the seven of them spend all of their time. They talked wistfully about returning to Aleppo one day but, given the immense devastation there, they must know deep down that their home no longer exists: for now, it is just a dream.

Amina said that if she could, she'd contact a smuggler tomorrow and risk the treacherous journey to Europe, for a chance of getting a more skilled job that would allow her to send more money back to her family in Iraq, but she couldn't leave her son.

I also met families who had fled Mosul, in central Iraq: Christians and Yazidis who knew that Isis would kill them because of their faith; Muslims who knew that Isis were prepared to kill anyone and did not want to risk getting caught in the cross-fire.

One family had owned a car sales business and three homes. Now, however, three generations were living in three rooms, with the men queuing for hours for infrequent, casual labour and the women learning how to make clothes to supplement their meagre income.

They too talked fondly of Mosul's beauty and their desire to return home. But they know that while Isis occupy the city, infrastructure is being destroyed and thousands of make-shift bombs are being left as booby traps. Even if Mosul is recaptured from Isis, it is likely to be years, not months, before they can return home safely: years before there are schools for their children, hospitals they can rely on, and enough resources to rebuild their homes and businesses. In the meantime they are powerless, trapped, their lives on pause.

Political leaders are focused on securing a military victory over Isis, which is of course important. But when it comes to improving people's lives and security in Iraq, this is just a starting point, not the end. Meeting Iraq's immediate humanitarian needs will cost at least $861 million, according to UN estimates. So far donors have committed just 9% of this. Without this money, vulnerable people will not receive shelter, water, food or healthcare, potentially triggering a humanitarian catastrophe in a once well-off country.

More funding will also be needed for years to come to support the process of de-mining areas that Isis leave, to rebuild homes, roads and basic services and help people get back on their feet. Without sufficient support from the international community, conditions will be rife for new strands of extremism, perhaps in a similar mould to Isis, to flourish again.

But physical infrastructure is much easier to rebuild than the social infrastructure ruined by war. Many people I met mentioned feeling betrayed by neighbours, or afraid of persecution on ethnic, religious or political grounds. Rebuilding trust takes time, so the process of reconciliation will require great leadership from within Iraq and outside it.

If I'm honest, it was difficult to avoid slipping into despair and despondency while in Iraq. With its complex problems, I expected people to have lost hope and indeed, some sadly had. But I was repeatedly struck by their dignity in the face of adversity: no act of human kindness, however small, was wasted. By providing food, medicines and training to refugee families and displaced people, and by working to defeat the ideology of extremism in future generations, Christian Aid's partners were providing small glimmers of hope in a dark place.

Let's ensure that Iraq doesn't become another 'forgotten crisis'' Even if the fighting ends, the international community must turn the money currently being spent on military efforts to repairing the damage done and to building a peaceful, secure Iraq – for the sake of these and many, many other families.

Since the defeat of ISIS some IDPs have now started to return. It is estimated that more than 1.5million IDPs in Iraq will return to their homes in this year. It is vital that any such returns are voluntary and meet international standards, i.e. that they are voluntary, safe, dignified, informed, preserve family unity, non-discriminatory, and sustainable. While some returns have been voluntary there are multiple reports of forced evictions and returns of IDPs, including to areas which are not yet safe to return to. The ancient and diverse city of Mosul has been left in ruins by months of ground fighting and aerial bombing. The infrastructural damage is only the tip of the ice-berg of the problem of rebuilding however; even when the homes, schools, hospitals, roads and shops are standing again, the impact on the people, and in particular the children, who lived under ISIS control or fled and endured the calamity of displacement, remains. As well as the loss of livelihoods and education, families displaced by the crisis have been tainted by association with ISIS and many fear returning to their homes for this reason. Next week, Kuwait will host a donor conference to raise funds for the reconstruction of Iraq. Any future funding towards the reconstruction of Iraq must consider the rebuilding of this kind of social capital as well as the physical rebuilding of damaged infrastructure to try and ensure a lasting peace.

28 March 2016

⇨ The above information is reprinted with kind permission from Christian Aid. Please visit www.christianaid.org.uk for further information.

Yemen: the forgotten war

An extract from an article by Amnesty International. Over the past two years the world has turned its back on a growing crisis.

A spiralling conflict

On 25 March 2015, an international coalition led by Saudi Arabia launched air strikes against the Huthi armed group in Yemen sparking a full-blown armed conflict.

Over the following two years, the conflict has spread and fighting has engulfed the entire country. Horrific human rights abuses, as well as war crimes, are being committed throughout the country causing unbearable suffering for civilians.

As well as relentless bombardment by coalition forces from the air, there is a battle being fought on the ground between rival factions. On one side are the Huthis, an armed group whose members belong to a branch of Shi'a Islam known as Zayidism. The Huthis are allied with supporters of Yemen's former President Ali Abdullah Saleh. On the other side are anti-Huthi forces that are allied with the current President Abd Rabbu Mansour Hadi and the Saudi Arabian-led coalition. Civilians are trapped in the middle – more than 12,000 of them have been killed and injured, and a humanitarian crisis has spiralled.

For two years, much of the world has ignored this raging conflict and heard little about its devastating consequences.

Civilians paying a heavy price

Civilians bear the brunt of the violence in Yemen. As well as causing the deaths and injuries of civilians, the conflict has exacerbated an already severe humanitarian crisis resulting from years of poverty and poor governance causing immense human suffering.

Approximately 18.8 million Yemenis today rely on humanitarian assistance in order to survive. In order to deny supplies to the Huthi forces, the coalition imposed a partial aerial and naval blockade. This is severely limiting the import and provision of fuel and other essentials, obstructing access to food, water, humanitarian assistance

and medical supplies and causing food prices to soar, creating a desperate situation for millions of people. Damage to key logistical infrastructure, including bridges, airports and seaports, from air strikes has also severely hampered the movement of crucial humanitarian supplies.

> **"My son was 14 hours old when he died... the doctors told us he needed intensive care and oxygen... We took him to every hospital we possibly could before he finally died. I wanted to take him outside the city but there was no way out"**

The Huthi armed group and allied forces are also endangering the lives of thousands of civilians in the southern city of Ta'iz by limiting the entry of crucial medical supplies and food. Humanitarian workers also accuse the Huthis of excessively restricting their movement of goods and staff, and forcing some of their aid programmes to close.

Who is fighting whom?

On one side is the Huthi armed group, often referred to as the 'Popular Committees', which is supported by certain army units and armed groups loyal to former President Ali Abdullah Saleh"

> **The force of the explosion sent my sisters and mother flying five metres, killing them instantly. Hani's body was not dug out until 12 hours later. My father Faisal (60) was the only survivor"**

On the other side is the military coalition led by Saudi Arabia and supported by President Hadi, which has carried out air strikes and ground operations in Yemen. Members of the coalition include the United Arab Emirates, Bahrain, Kuwait, Qatar, Jordan and Sudan. The USA and UK have been providing key intelligence and logistical support to the coalition.

Human rights abuses by all sides

Amnesty International has gathered evidence revealing that all the parties to this conflict have committed serious violations of human rights and international humanitarian law, including war crimes.

"I was standing in the kitchen when I heard an explosion. Suddenly all I felt was something in my neck... I am now quadriplegic, paralysed from the neck down. That night, shrapnel entered my neck and exited through my seventh vertebrae. We had just moved to our new house, we thought we were safe. Who will take care of my family now?"

Amnesty International has documented 34 air strikes across six different governorates (Sana'a, Sa'da, Hajjah, Hodeidah, Ta'iz and Lahj) by the Saudi Arabia-led coalition that appear to have violated international humanitarian law – the rules that apply during a conflict which are sometimes known as the 'laws of war' – resulting in 494 civilian deaths (including at least 148 children) and 359 civilian injuries. These have included attacks that appear to have deliberately targeted civilians and civilian objects such as hospitals, schools, markets and mosques, which may amount to war crimes.

The Saudi Arabia-led coalition has also used cluster munitions, lethal explosive weapons banned under international law. When launched, cluster bombs release dozens – sometimes hundreds – of small 'bomblets', which often lie unexploded and can cause horrific injuries long after the initial attack. Amnesty International has documented the coalition's use of at least four different types of cluster munitions, including US, UK and Brazilian-manufactured models.

Imprecise weapons are used on a daily basis in residential areas, causing civilian casualties. Such indiscriminate attacks violate the laws of war.

Amnesty International has also investigated 30 ground attacks – by both pro and anti-Huthi forces – in Aden and Ta'iz which did not distinguish between combatants and civilians, and killed at least 68 civilians, most of whom were women and children. Fighters from both sides have also used imprecise weapons, such as artillery and mortar fire or Grad rockets, in heavily populated civilian areas and have operated in the midst of residential neighbourhoods, launching attacks from or near homes, schools and hospitals. All these attacks are serious violations of international humanitarian law and may amount to war crimes.

The Huthi armed group, supported by state security forces, has carried out a wave of arrests of its opponents, including human rights defenders, journalists and academics, arbitrarily seizing critics at gunpoint and subjecting some to enforced disappearance as part of a chilling campaign to quash dissent in areas of Yemen under its control.

The USA, UK, France, Spain, Canada and Turkey transferred nearly US$5.9 billion worth of arms to Saudi Arabia between 2015 and 2016, including drones, bombs, torpedoes, rockets and missiles, which risk being used to facilitate serious violations in Yemen.

Anti-Huthi forces allied to Yemen's President Hadi and the coalition, have also carried out a campaign of intimidation and harassment against hospital staff in Ta'iz and are endangering civilians by stationing fighters and military positions near medical facilities.

Arms fuelling the crisis

"The irresponsible and unlawful flow of arms to the warring parties in Yemen has directly contributed to civilian suffering on a mass scale. It's time for world leaders to stop putting their economic interests first"

James Lynch, Amnesty International

In the face of multiple reports pointing to reckless conduct in Yemen and the devastating impact of serious violations of international law on civilians, many countries have continued to sell and transfer weapons to Saudi Arabia and its coalition members for use in the conflict. Arms have also been diverted into the hands of Huthi and other armed groups fighting in Yemen.

Several of these states are parties to the Arms Trade Treaty which has the aim of "reducing human suffering" and which makes it unlawful to transfer weapons where there is a high risk they could be used to commit serious violations of international law.

Amnesty International is urging all states to ensure that no party to the conflict in Yemen is supplied – either directly or indirectly – with weapons, munitions, military equipment or technology that could be used in the conflict until they end such serious violations. This also applies to logistical and financial support for such transfers.

Urgent need for accountability

In such a context of lawlessness and abuse, there is an urgent need for truth, accountability and justice for victims of the conflict. Given the apparent inadequacies of Saudi Arabia and Yemen-led investigations to date, Amnesty International believes the only way to achieve this is through the establishment of a UN-led independent international investigation to look into alleged violations by all parties to the conflict with a view to ensuring that those responsible for crimes are brought to justice in fair trials and effective measures are taken to address the suffering of victims and their families and to help them rebuild their lives.

⇨ The above extract is reprinted with kind permission from Amnesty International. Please visit www.amnesty.org for further information.

© 2018 Amnesty International

A child is a child

An extract from the article *Protecting children on the move from violence, abuse and exploitation.*

EXECUTIVE SUMMARY

Millions of children are on the move across international borders – fleeing violence and conflict, disaster or poverty, in pursuit of a better life. Hundreds of thousands move on their own. When they encounter few opportunities to move legally, children resort to dangerous routes and engage smugglers to help them cross borders. Serious gaps in the laws, policies and services meant to protect children on the move further leave them bereft of protection and care. Deprived, unprotected and often alone, children on the move can become easy prey for traffickers and others who abuse and exploit them.

Alarming numbers of children are moving alone

Many children move alone and face particularly grave risks. In parts of the world, the number of children moving on their own has skyrocketed. On the dangerous Central Mediterranean Sea passage from North Africa to Europe, 92 per cent of children who arrived in Italy in 2016 and the first two months of 2017 were unaccompanied, up from 75 per cent in 2015. At least 300,000 unaccompanied and separated children moving across borders were registered in 80 countries in 2015–2016 – a near fivefold increase from 66,000 in 2010–2011. The total number of unaccompanied and separated children on the move worldwide is likely much higher.

Specific reasons motivate children to undertake journeys alone. Many seek to reunite with family members already abroad. Others pursue their families' aspirations for this generation to have a better life. Perceptions of the potential benefits of children moving, especially to certain destinations, filter through social networks. Other factors include family breakdown, domestic violence, child marriage and forced conscription.

Without safe and legal pathways, children's journeys are rife with risk and exploitation

Whatever their motivation, children often find few opportunities to move legally. Family reunification, humanitarian visas, refugee resettlement spots, and work or study visas are out of reach for most. But barriers to legal migration do not stop people from moving, they only push them underground.

Wherever families and children desperate to move encounter barriers, smuggling in human beings thrives. Smugglers range from people helping others in need for a fee to organised

A surge in the numbers of children seeking asylum in Europe

Child asylum seekers

2008

2016

For children, this trend was even more dramatic. Their numbers increased almost tenfold compared to 2008 and fourfold compared to 2013.

Source: Eurostat, <http://ec.europa.eu.eurostat/web/asylum-and-manged-migration/data/database>

criminal networks that deliver children into hazardous and exploitative situations.

Once children and families place their fates in the hands of smugglers, the transaction can readily take a turn towards abuse or exploitation – especially when children and families incur debts to pay smugglers' fees. Europol estimates that 20 per cent of suspected smugglers on their radar have ties to human trafficking – they help children cross borders, only to sell them into exploitation, sometimes akin to contemporary forms of slavery.

Some routes are particularly rife with risks. In a recent International Organization for Migration survey, over three-quarters of 1,600 children aged 14–17 who arrived in Italy via the Central Mediterranean route reported experiences such as being held against their will or being forced to work without pay at some point during their journeys – indications that they may have been trafficked or otherwise exploited. Traffickers and other exploiters thrive especially where state institutions are weak, where organised crime abounds, and also where migrants become stuck and desperate.

As States struggle to manage migration, children fall through the cracks

As large numbers of refugees and migrants arrive, children among them are routinely left in conditions that would be deemed unacceptable for native-born children. They languish in overcrowded shelters, end up in makeshift camps or are left exposed to the dangers of life on the streets. Sometimes, compatriots force them to work under exploitative conditions in exchange for shelter and food. Mistrust of authorities and fear of detention and deportation keep children from coming forward to seek protection and support.

Harsh border enforcement policies leave children in limbo and exacerbate their risk of exploitation

Border closures and aggressive pushback measures can leave children and their families stranded in countries where they do not want to stay, are not welcome, or have few prospects. Unable to move on or go back, they are trapped in prolonged limbo that feeds anxiety, despair and self-harm, as documented among children in Greece and in Australian processing facilities in Nauru.

Some children avoid authorities for fear of detention, living on the streets under abysmal conditions and sometimes selling sex or resorting to petty crime as they save up to pay smugglers to facilitate their onward journeys.

Children on the move are children, first and foremost – they need protection

The Convention on the Rights of the Child protects every child, everywhere. All children, regardless of legal status, nationality or statelessness, have the right to be protected from harm, obtain such essential services as health care and education, be with their families, and have their best interests guide decisions that affect them.

Yet in practice, children on the move often suffer violations of their rights because of their migrant status. The way children on the move are treated varies widely from State to State, and the responsibility to care for them often falls too heavily on poorer countries. Even children fleeing violence and conflict often do not get the protection they need, particularly when refugee protection is curtailed in law or practice.

Sharing, not shifting, the responsibility to protect children on the move

The current system is failing refugee and migrant children. States have a responsibility to uphold their rights and protect all children within their borders, without exception.

When world leaders adopted the New York Declaration for Refugees and Migrants in September 2016, they acknowledged the urgent and unmet needs of vulnerable child migrants – especially unaccompanied and separated children – who do not qualify for international protection as refugees and who may need assistance.

It is now time to act.

Children's rights are not confined by national borders. Where conflict

---

A surge in the numbers of children seeking asylum in Europe

Child asylum seekers

2008

2016

The share of children among asylum seekers increased by almost half, from one in five in 2008 to one in three in 2016.

Source: Eurostat, <http://ec.europa.eu.eurostat/web/asylum-and-manged-migration/data/database>

The number of refugees under UNHCR's mandate – half of whom are children – rose by 59 per cent between 2011 and 2016

The total number of refugees has increased by **59%** over the last five years, from **10.4 million** to **16.5 million**.

Half of all **refugees are children** under the age of 18. In 2015, globally, 8.2 million children under the age of 18 living outside their countries of birth were refugees.

Source: UNICEF analysis based on United Nations High Commissioner for Refugees. Population Statistics Database. UNHCR, 2016: Mid-Year Trends 2016. UNHCR, Geneva, 2017.

or disaster, neglect, abuse or marginalisation drive children to move, their rights move with them. Leadership is urgently required to forge global agreement on how to protect and guarantee the rights of children as they move, no matter who or where they are.

Why children migrate

Children migrate to escape violence, armed conflict and persecution; the ravages of climate change and natural disasters; and poverty and inequality – and to pursue their aspirations for a better life. Their reasons for migrating may evolve and overlap. Migration can be a way to exercise agency and cope with drastically constrained choices, and it can bring benefits to those who undertake it – and to the societies they leave and join.

There are some distinctive aspects to children's migration that contribute to the high and rising numbers of children moving on their own. Many young migrants set out to find opportunities for work or education. In other cases, children leave home to avoid the prospect of unwanted child marriage, female genital mutilation or gender-based violence (in the case of girls) or forced conscription (a particular risk for boys in some contexts). Women and girls usually have less control over the decision to migrate than men and boys; for the former, the decision is more likely to be made by their families rather than through their own agency.

Family looms large among the factors that motivate children's migration. Some children migrate when their families break down or their parents die. Others move to join family members who made the journey ahead of them. A significant proportion of unaccompanied children moving northward from Central America, for instance, have at least one parent or other close relative already residing in the United States.

In some cases, children migrate on their own because their chances of success are deemed greater than those of older family members. Interviews conducted in Afghanistan, among communities from which unaccompanied migrant children originated, revealed that decisions to migrate were informed by an awareness that children under 18 arriving in Europe or Australia would enjoy special protections and would have a greater chance of being allowed to stay.

Since 1990, the number of international child migrants has grown along with the global population, with the share of migrants among the world's children remaining stable. Movements related to conflict, meanwhile, have spiked. The overall number of refugees – children and adults under the mandate of the United Nations High Commissioner for Refugees (UNHCR) – increased from 10.4 million at the end of 2011 to 16.5 million in 2016. While in 2005 about one in 350 children was a refugee, in 2015 the ratio came to

nearly one in 200 children. Half the world's refugees were children.

Alarming numbers of children are moving on their own. On the Central Mediterranean route to Italy in 2015, unaccompanied and separated children made up 75 per cent of all children arriving in Italy by sea; this proportion rose to 92 per cent in 2016 and remained at that level through the first two months of 2017. Most of these children came from Eritrea, the Gambia, Nigeria, Egypt and Guinea.

Around 200,000 unaccompanied and separated children applied for asylum in 2015 and 2016 in about 80 countries with available data while about 100,000 were apprehended at the border between Mexico and the United States during the same period. Taken together, these numbers – 300,000 children – demonstrate a dramatic rise, compared to the 66,000 recorded in 2010–2011. These numbers refer to only a subset of children moving across borders on their own. The total number of unaccompanied and separated children on the move worldwide is likely much higher.

May 2017

⇨ The above extract is reprinted with kind permission from Unicef UK from the report *A child is a child*. Please visit www.unicef.org.uk for further information.

Nearly a quarter of the world's school-age children live in crisis-hit countries

Unicef Goodwill Ambassador Orlando Bloom visits conflict-hit Ukraine to highlight the importance of education in emergencies.

Unicef Goodwill Ambassador Orlando Bloom travelled to conflict-hit eastern Ukraine as a new report reveals nearly a quarter of the world's school-aged children live in crisis-hit countries.

Bloom visited classrooms hit by shells just three kilometres from the frontline of the conflict that broke out more than two years ago. Approximately 580,000 children are in urgent need of aid and more than 230,000 children have been forced from their homes. Around one in five schools and kindergartens in the region have been damaged or destroyed and around 300,000 children are in immediate need of assistance to continue their education.

The trip came as new findings show that nearly a quarter of the world's school-aged children – 462 million – now live in countries affected by crisis.

"I met children like 11-year-old Liana who hid in the basement of their school for almost two weeks, in freezing conditions, without lighting or heat, while shelling devastated the classrooms above," said Orlando Bloom, who first travelled to see Unicef's work in 2007. "Now, after surviving some of the most terrifying experiences life could possibly throw at them, all they want is to get back to the safety and routine of school and plan for their futures."

The Education Cannot Wait proposal, written by the Overseas Development Institute and commissioned by a range of partners including Unicef, reveals that nearly one in six – or 75 million – children from pre-primary to upper-secondary age (3–18) living in nations affected by crises is classed as being in desperate need of educational support. However, on average, only two per cent of global humanitarian appeals are dedicated to education.

At the very first World Humanitarian Summit in Istanbul in less than three weeks' time, a groundbreaking new fund – Education Cannot Wait – will be launched to give access to learning to every child in need in emergencies. It aims to raise nearly $4 billion to reach 13.6 million children in need of education in emergencies within five years, before reaching 75 million children by 2030.

"Education changes lives in emergencies," said Josephine Bourne, Unicef's Global Chief of Education. "Going to school keeps children safe from abuses like trafficking and recruitment into armed groups and is a vital investment in children's futures and in the future of their communities. It is time education is prioritised by the international community as an essential part of basic humanitarian response, alongside water, food and shelter."

In eastern Ukraine, and in emergencies across the world, Unicef is working around the clock to get children back to learning – to keep them safe and secure their futures. Unicef so far has supported the repair and rehabilitation of 57 schools in eastern Ukraine and has supplied hundreds of thousands of children with vital supplies like schoolbooks, desks and pencils, as well as psychological support and catch-up classes. Unicef has also reached nearly 280,000 children with information on the risks posed by land mines and unexploded ordnance, which litter communities near the frontline.

"For too many children in eastern Ukraine, simply walking to school could end their life, or result in life-changing injuries," said Giovanna Barberis, Unicef representative in Ukraine. "Since the beginning of the crisis, more than 55,000 unexploded landmines, shells and other ordnance have been found and removed – and we know this is just the tip of the iceberg. Our aim is to ensure that all children can safely get to class, study and play."

During his time in eastern Ukraine, Bloom also met with schoolchildren who are receiving counselling from Unicef-supported psychologists, to help them recover from their distressing experiences during the conflict.

"Education is providing children in eastern Ukraine with the building blocks to rebuild their lives in a safe and supportive environment," said Bloom. "Every child in humanitarian emergencies deserves a fair chance of a bright future."

Across the world, more than 37 million primary and lower secondary children are out of school and educational facilities are continually forced to close as a consequence of conflicts and of natural disasters – putting millions more at risk. In Syria alone, more than 6,000 schools are out of use – attacked, occupied by the military or taken over as an emergency shelter. In North-East Nigeria and Cameroon more than 1,800 schools have been shut due to the crisis and in conflict-hit Central African Republic a quarter of schools are not functioning.

Unicef UK is urging the UK Government to sign up to the Safe Schools Declaration, sending a clear message to the world that schools must not be attacked or occupied for military purposes.

4 May 2016

⇨ The above information is reprinted with kind permission from Politics Home. Please visit www.politicshome.com for further information.

International laws and child rights

Over the past 40 years, international law has developed to better protect children from military exploitation.

In 1977, the Additional Protocols to the 1949 Geneva Conventions prohibited the military recruitment and use of children under the age of 15, which is now recognised as a war crime under the Rome Statute of the International Criminal Court (2002). It applies to both government-controlled armed forces and non-state armed groups.

The prohibition on the use of children under 15 was reaffirmed in the Convention on the Rights of the Child (1989), which also defined a child for the first time as any person under the age of 18.

The standard was raised again by the Optional Protocol to the Convention on the Rights of the Child on the involvement of children in armed conflict, also known as OPAC (2000). OPAC was the world's first international treaty wholly focused on ending the military exploitation of children. The treaty prohibits the conscription of children under the age of 18 and their participation in hostilities. It also prohibits the voluntary recruitment of children by non-state armed groups, although it allows state armed forces to recruit from age 16, as long as the children recruited are not sent to war.

Most states have now signed OPAC, which is (slowly) driving the world towards a de facto ban on the use of children in warfare. But the double-standard that applies to state and non-state recruitment of children is hampering international efforts to persuade non-state armed groups to release the children they have recruited.

Nonetheless, states that sign OPAC can commit to a higher recruitment age if they wish to do so, which then cannot be lowered. Most states have done this. Two-thirds of the world's governments now only allow the military recruitment of adult volunteers from age 18. Among those that have so far resisted this are the US (which recruits from age 17) and the UK (which recruits from age 16). Both had insisted on the OPAC double-standard at the time of its negotiation.

Other international laws have also helped to raise standards. For example, the International Labour Organization's Worst Forms of Child Labour Convention 182 (1999) also prohibits compulsory enlistment below the age of 18. The African Union's Charter on the Rights and Welfare of the Child (1999) prohibits state armed forces from recruiting volunteers under the age of 18.

Our impact

Child Soldiers International evolved from a coalition of organisations, which worked together to bring OPAC into being, by building international support for it, helping to draft it, and ensuring it was widely adopted. Today we campaign for the universal adoption of OPAC, we support UN bodies to hold governments to account on their commitments, and we engage with governments themselves to encourage rising standards, so that fewer children are subject to military exploitation. We are also training governments, parliamentarians, armed forces and communities around the world on OPAC and its practical implementation. We complement this work by working with community and civil society organisations in conflict affected countries. Together, we develop and deliver practical initiatives which prevent child soldier recruitment, and support the effective reintegration of former child soldiers'.

⇨ The above information is reprinted with kind permission from Child Soldiers International. Please visit www.child-soldiers.org for further information.

© 2018 Child Soldiers International

A shocking number of kids are fighting and dying for ISIS

The use of child fighters creates a horrifying dilemma for forces battling the militant group.

By Charlotte Alfred

The so-called Islamic State group is recruiting children and sending them to die on the battlefields of Syria and Iraq at an "increasing and unprecedented rate", according to a new study of the group's propaganda.

The survey from Georgia State University academics analyzed 89 images of children and youth who the extremist group said had been killed while carrying out militant operations between 1 January 2015 and 31 January 2016.

These children were among some 1,500 young people that the militants have enlisted to fight, said Mia Bloom, one of the study authors. She estimated that there are likely thousands more children who are being indoctrinated by the militants and could serve as potential recruits.

"This study is hinting at the fact that the problems are much greater than we ever imagined," Bloom said of the report, published Friday by *CTC Sentinel*, the journal of the military academy West Point's Counter Terrorism Center.

The study finds 21 children died in suicide attacks using explosive-packed vehicles in the first seven months of 2015 – two-and-a-half times the previous estimate. In fact, the rate of child casualties seems to be accelerating. Last January, six children died in suicide operations for the militant group. This January, the toll rose to 11 children, and the number of suicide bombings involving children tripled from a year ago.

This disturbing trend is likely to continue, say the study authors. As it loses territory, ISIS may resort to more suicide attacks and ambushes, two of the most common causes of child deaths in the survey, they said. Militant groups tend to use these types of attacks when on the defensive, either out of desperation or as a form of psychological warfare.

The militant group has forced, intimidated and recruited children into its ranks since its early days in Iraq, according to the United Nations. As the group expanded into Syria, split from al-Qaeda and seized a wide stretch of territory in the region in 2014, its use of child fighters has swelled.

ISIS captured hundreds of children, especially Yazidis, during its advance. In territories under the group's brutal control, fighters indoctrinate and recruit children through the school system and by desensitising them to violence with public beheadings and crucifixions. Foreign fighters who have flocked to the region from Europe, Africa and the Middle East sometimes bring their children along to fight, too.

While an exact figure is hard to assess, one group reported that 1,100 children were recruited as fighters between January and August last year. Bloom estimates that at least 1,500 children are currently part of the core group of fighters. Friday's study sheds some light on who these young recruits are.

Of the 89 children killed since January 2015, 31 per cent were Syrian and 11 per cent were Iraqi. A further 25 per cent came from one of those two countries but it wasn't clear which. Others came from Yemen, Saudi Arabia, Tunisia, Libya, the United Kingdom, France, Australia and Nigeria.

Most of the children – 60 percent – were determined to be between the ages of 12 and 16. Six per cent were under 12 years old. The United Nations previously reported that children as young as eight were trained to fight in ISIS military camps.

Children who escaped the group's clutches have described long, gruelling months at military camps. "I saw a lot of people being tortured," a 14-year-old former child fighter told *The WorldPost* last year. "Every day they whipped people, even the children. Nobody was allowed to leave."

The use of child soldiers is a global problem – and one that is on the rise in war-torn countries like Yemen and South Sudan.

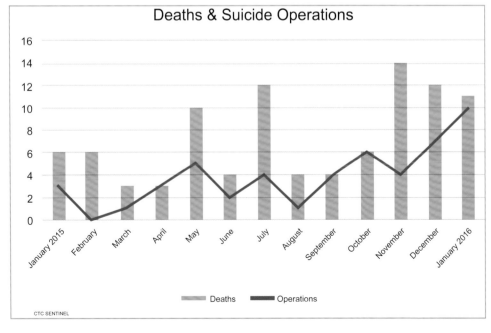

Deaths & Suicide Operations

Legend: Deaths, Operations

CTC SENTINEL

But ISIS differs from other militant groups in the way it uses children as fighters, the study found.

While other groups have deployed children to make up for a shortage of adult fighters or for specific tasks (like attacking civilian targets), ISIS uses kids in a very similar way to adult fighters. The study found child fighters were dying in broadly the same locations and types of attacks as adults were.

"Children are fighting alongside, rather than in lieu of, adult males," the study says. "The use of children and youth has been normalised under the Islamic State's rule."

This poses a horrifying dilemma for local and international forces fighting to combat ISIS.

US forces fighting the militant group "need to be able to make a nuanced distinction between a child, and a child who might be dangerous," Bloom said. "American police can't even do that in our cities... The possibility for error is great, and the backlash could be horrific."

Further, the scale and methods of ISIS' youth recruitment make it even more complicated to help children who escape – either during combat or in a future where the militant group is defeated. In other conflicts, religious institutions and children's families play a critical role in reintegrating them into society, Bloom said. But with ISIS, the families are often implicated in their recruitment and the religious indoctrination runs very deep.

"We're talking about taking children away from their parents, who have exposed them to this ideology and put them in danger, which is very challenging," she said.

19 February 2016

⇨ The above information is reprinted with kind permission from *Huffington Post*. Please visit www. huffingtonpost.com for further information.

Israel's armed forces and grave violations of children's rights

Today, the UN Human Rights Council held a general debate on the situation in the occupied Palestinian territories. On this occasion, Defence for Children International – Palestine delivered an oral statement to raise concerns over the grave violations of Palestinian children's rights, including the use of administrative detention and solitary confinement, and shared key recommendations.

Please find the statement hereunder:

Israel has the dubious distinction of being the only country in the world that systematically prosecutes between 500 and 700 children each year in military courts lacking fundamental fair trial rights.

Amid heightened violence in the autumn of 2015, the number of Palestinian children detained in the Israeli prison system skyrocketed. At the end of March 2016, 444 Palestinian children were in the Israeli prison system, the highest known total since January 2008 when the Israel Prison Service (IPS) began sharing data. The IPS has stopped consistently releasing data since May 2016.

In 2016, DCIP collected affidavits from 158 West Bank children detained by Israeli forces and prosecuted under the jurisdiction of Israeli military courts. The data shows that 62 per cent of children endured some form of physical violence following arrest and 52 per cent were verbally abused, intimidated or threatened.

Of the 158 children, 25 were held in solitary confinement for an average period of 16 days for interrogation purposes, an alarming increase over the previous year. The longest period of isolation for a child that DCIP documented in 2016 was 29 days.

In October 2015, Israel renewed the practice of administrative detention against Palestinian children in the West Bank for the first time in four years. Administrative detention is the imprisonment of individuals by the state for prolonged periods without charge or trial and based on secret evidence.

DCIP has documented the use of administrative detention against 14 children in 2016. Five Palestinian children were placed in administrative detention following accusations of inciting or threatening to commit violence in Facebook posts.

Additionally, Israeli forces and security guards killed 32 Palestinian children in the occupied West Bank, including East Jerusalem, in 2016, making it the deadliest year of the past decade for West Bank children.

Defence for Children International urges all members of the Human Rights Council to:

Demand that Israeli authorities immediately stop the use of administrative detention orders against Palestinian children and enshrine this prohibition in law;

Condemn Israeli forces' use of excessive force against Palestinians the occupied West Bank, including East Jerusalem; and

Demand that Israeli forces at all times act in accordance with the UN Basic Principles on the Use of Force and Firearms by Law Enforcement Officials (1990).

19 June 2017

⇨ The above information is reprinted with kind permission from Defence for Children International. Please visit www.defenceforchildren.org for further information.

Ending the recruitment and use of children in armed conflict

An extract from an article from Unicef.

INTRODUCTION

Some 20 years ago, international humanitarian advocate Graça Machel released her ground breaking _Report on the Impact of Armed Conflict on Children_. It became a _cri de coeur_, drawing the attention of governments, child protection agencies and civil society. The former First Lady of Mozambique and South Africa compelled States to confront the fact that children were being used as weapons of war, and the phrase 'child soldiers' became a rallying call for action.

The international community called for an end to the outrage and recommended actions to protect children from recruitment and use by armed forces and armed groups. Almost a generation later, this report sets out areas where important progress has been made towards ending the recruitment and use of children in conflict, including through the Children, Not Soldiers campaign, and makes recommendations for action by governments.

Despite considerable progress, however, tens of thousands of children – boys and girls under the age of 18 – are still estimated to be recruited and used in conflicts worldwide. As many as 16,000 children in South Sudan alone have been recruited and used by armed forces and groups since the start of the conflict in December 2013, and all parties to the current conflict on the ground in Yemen have engaged in widespread recruitment of children. As long as these grave violations continue, the international community has not honoured its promise to end, once and for all, the recruitment and use of children in armed conflict.

Children are used for various functions by armed forces and groups, including but not limited to, fighters, cooks, porters, messengers and spies, or they are subjected to sexual exploitation.

Some children are abducted or forcibly recruited, while others are driven to join by poverty, by circumstances of political or social exclusion, or the desire to seek revenge for violence committed against them or their families. In all cases the conscription of children for military purposes and their use by armed forces or groups is a grave violation of their rights.

The Optional Protocol to the Convention on the Rights of the Child on the involvement of children in armed conflict (2000) requires States to ensure that children under age 18 are not compulsorily recruited into their armed forces. Additionally, it requires them to raise the minimum age for voluntary recruitment to above age 15. It also forbids anyone under 18 to participate in hostilities. States are also required to take all feasible measures to prevent recruitment and use of individuals under the age of 18 by non-State armed groups. And yet, despite the clear directives of this legal instrument, and the fact that some 176 countries have either ratified or signed it, the recruitment and use of child soldiers continues.

In adopting the Sustainable Development Goals in 2015, governments around the world agreed to end the recruitment and use of child soldiers and fulfil the provisions of the Optional Protocol. Specifically, Target 8.7 compels States to take immediate and effective measures to "secure the prohibition and elimination of the worst forms of child labour, including the recruitment and use of child soldiers, and by 2025 end child labour in all its forms". Adding to these clear mandates for change are no fewer than 11 United Nations Security Council resolutions aimed at preventing and ending grave child rights violations in armed conflict. In addition this year, the international community will come together at the first ever World Humanitarian Summit with a focus on the safety and protection of civilians.

> ## "I was armed with a gun. At the time, nothing affected me because I was taking drugs. I wasn't thinking straight. Even if you were scared you couldn't leave [the group]"
>
> **Isma, a 14-year-old girl who joined an armed group in the Central African Republic**

With the legal frameworks set and moral imperatives clear, it is now time to turn goals and promises into action. With political will mustered and international support provided, 2016 could be the pivotal year for making urgently needed progress.

Children continue to be recruited and abducted by armed forces and groups

Currently seven government-armed forces are listed in the Secretary-General's annual report on _Children and Armed Conflict_ for recruitment and use of children. However, 49 armed groups are listed for that grave violation.

Child recruitment is occurring through forced recruitment, including abduction, as well as through the use of new means such as social media for recruitment. Some contemporary armed groups are known to employ recruitment strategies that specifically target children. In his 2015 report on children and armed conflict, the United Nations Secretary-General indicates that 49 of the 57 parties to armed conflict that are listed as perpetrators of violations against children are non-State armed groups. For example, in Iraq and the Syrian Arab Republic, the proliferation of armed groups and the military advances by ISIL have made children even more vulnerable to recruitment. Children as young as age 12 are undergoing military training as well as being used as informants and guards at checkpoints and other strategic locations. Armed groups in other conflicts are also abducting children, including groups in Afghanistan, the Democratic Republic of the Congo, Nigeria, Somalia and South Sudan.

Over the past decade, the number of extremely violent conflicts almost doubled. Globally, the rise in high intensity conflicts has hit children hard. One United Nations report described egregious violations against children. Some children, for example were "forced to witness or take part in beheadings, immolations and summary executions. They were also indoctrinated, recruited and forced to be suicide bombers or human shields. Girls were subjected to additional abuses, including sexual slavery, abduction and forced marriage… Such brutal tactics had severe repercussions on children, which will have lasting effects for generations to come."

The progress being made with government armies towards ending the recruitment and use of children is harder to achieve with non-State armed groups.

Further, serious security considerations impact the ability of child protection actors and agencies to engage with some non-State-armed groups.

However, agreements have been reached with several non-State-armed groups that have led to the prevention of child recruitment and to the release of child soldiers. These non-State groups include the Cobra Faction in South Sudan, the Moro Islamic Liberation Front in the Philippines, and several armed groups in Myanmar. Such agreements show that concerted action can end the recruitment and use of children in armed conflicts.

Children allegedly associated with armed groups are detained and treated as security threats, deprived of their rights and protections

A large number of children alleged to be associated with armed groups are being arrested and detained, deprived of their liberty and treated as security threats. Instead of being viewed as threats and deprived of their rights, children who are vulnerable to recruitment by armed forces and groups should be supported in their release and reintegration. Detention can have a profound and negative impact on children's long-term physical, emotional and cognitive development. In Afghanistan, for example, some children who were alleged to be associated with armed groups and detained in correction centres have been found to experience deep depression. Many need psychosocial support, including those who suffer further violence in the centres, such as sexual abuse.

Information about the situation of such child detainees is often difficult to obtain. In one example, in Somalia, more than 75 children alleged to

have been associated with the non-State-armed group Al-Shabaab were detained at a government 'Rehabilitation Centre' for a few years. Many of the children were placed together with adult detainees and prevented from contacting their families. Humanitarian access was denied until August 2014. In September 2015, following multilateral negotiations, 79 children were handed over to Unicef and its implementing partners. They were subsequently reunited with their families or provided with interim care, while also benefiting from the community-based socio-economic reintegration programme.

⇨ The above extract is reprinted with kind permission from Unicef UK from the report *Ending the recruitment of children in armed conflict*. Please visit www.unicef.org.uk for further information.

© 2018 UNICEF

Rape, murder, forced marriage: what girls in conflict zones get instead of education

***An extract from an article from* The Conversation.**

By Pauline Rose, Professor, International Education and Director, Research for Equitable Access and Learning Centre, University of Cambridge

THE CONVERSATION

Education is life-changing for children and young people, but the power of education is systematically ignored in situations of humanitarian crisis – and never more than at present. This neglect is reflected in the tiny amount allocated to children's schooling in humanitarian responses: it involves only 2% of humanitarian funding. This neglect affects the lives of a generation of children and young people forever – once their education is disrupted it can never be retrieved.

Progress towards recognising education as part of a humanitarian response has been slow and the crisis has been worsening – resulting in millions more children and young people who are missing the chance to go to school. There are now more displaced people than ever before – and around half of refugees are children.

And while the media is focused on the plight of families whose lives have been ruined by conflict in Syria, in other parts of the world millions of people have spent many years away from home. Dadaab, in northern Kenya, is the world's largest refugee camp and has been in existence for more than 23 years. Strikingly, there are more than 10,000 third-generation refugees in Dadaab, born to parents who were also born in the camps. Yet, while inhabitants of the camps see the importance of education as the only thing they can take home, until recently there were no secondary school opportunities for the vast majority of young people there.

The World Humanitarian Summit in Istanbul must be a turning point in giving prominence to education for those caught up in conflict for the sake of this and future generations of children and young people.

Adolescent girls suffer most

Adolescent girls' education journeys are being blocked in four key ways. First, with just 13% of the extremely small pot of UNHCR education funding allocated to secondary schooling, it is no surprise that just 4% of the poorest girls in conflict affected areas complete secondary school. As a result, adolescent girls in conflict zones are 90% more likely to be out of school than elsewhere.

These girls are not only invisible casualties – they also often become targets. Unsafe journeys to school and direct attacks on school buildings mean that for many girls, most famously Malala Yousafzai, fulfilling their right to go to schooling means risking their lives.

Not only have attacks on schools increased 17-fold between 2000 and 2014, but there have been three times as many attacks on girls' schools than boys' schools in recent years. It takes just one day to destroy a school, but will take years to rebuild. In Syria alone 25% of schools have been destroyed, damaged or occupied since the conflict started.

Even their journeys to school place young girls at risk of physical and sexual violence. More than half of adolescent girls in the Democratic Republic of Congo report experiencing physical violence. And while all the 51 countries affected by conflict since 1985 have reported sexual violence cases against adolescent girls, less than 4% of the funding requested by aid agencies accounts for programmes to tackle gender-based violence. In these situations, saving lives is inseparable from changing lives through education.

Limited opportunities

Early marriage is also a frequent alternative to education in contexts of severely limited opportunities and unsafe journeys to school. More than half of the 30 countries with the highest rate of child marriage are fragile or affected by conflict. And the transitions can be sudden – there were 18 times more early marriages among Syrian refugees in Jordan in 2013 compared with 2011.

A lack of education can also result in girls being recruited to fight in armed forces. While figures are hard to come by, on one estimate, around 40% of child soldiers are young women. Once recruited, their lives are disposable, three-quarters of suicide bombers in some West African countries have been identified as young women. And military and terrorist organisations abduct young women: in Chibok, northern Nigeria, Boko Haram abducted at least 276 girls – at least 219 of them are still missing.

Education cannot wait

There is an urgent need to remove the obstacles facing adolescent girls on their journey to school. The shocking statistics presented here provide clear evidence of a problem that can no longer be ignored. Facing up to the problem needs to be accompanied by taking action.

The launch of the Education Cannot Wait Fund at the World Humanitarian

Summit next week is a golden opportunity for world leaders to show their commitment to transforming the lives of children and young people for the future.

But realising change is not just about grand gestures at world summits. As commitments we have made together with others as part of the US First Lady's Let Girls' Learn Initiative highlight, change has to happen on the ground. Changing journeys of adolescent girls requires working together with communities to ensure they finally get the education they deserve.

20 May 2016

⇨ The above extract is reprinted with kind permission from *The Conversation*. Please visit www.theconversation.com for further information.

The shocking story of one-year-old Ali

In April 2017, one-year-old Ali and his family were used as human shields in Mosul, Iraq. Caught in a bombing, Ali was severely injured and both his parents and brother were killed. The baby boy is currently being treated at a hospital south of Mosul. His aunt and uncle are taking care of him and Khaled, a Handicap International physiotherapist, is supporting Ali's recovery.

In Qayyarah hospital, the heat is stifling. Mosquito nets have been installed over each bed, to protect patients from the hundreds of flies buzzing around the ceiling. In the women and children's room, a dozen beds are lined up, one by the other. Somewhere, a baby is crying.

Through one of the mosquito nets, you can make out the silhouette of a young woman holding a little boy in her arms. Khaled, Handicap International's physiotherapist, walks toward the bed and the baby's cries gradually stop. Ali, intrigued, looks at Khaled.

"How is he today?" asks the physiotherapist to the young woman holding the baby. "He's feeling very hot and his leg hurts, but he's strong and he'll recover," says Kitba, looking tenderly at her nephew.

Just a few months ago, little Ali was still living in Mosul, with his brother, sister and parents. But then the unimaginable happened.

"One day, as we were all sitting at home, armed men came to take us," says Kitba. "They gathered us with other inhabitants of our neighbourhood and took us to a school, to use us as human shields. Bombings soon started… and Ali's parents died instantly; his older brother too, who was only nine years old."

Ali's grandparents, uncle and aunt survived the bombings and fled, carrying Ali and his sister in their arms.

"As we were running towards an army-controlled area, bombings kept getting stronger. It was as if it would never stop. My dad was so scared that he had a stroke. We were brought to a field hospital and then transferred here, in Qayyarah, a few days ago."

Long and difficult road ahead

As Kitba recalls their escape, Ali plays with an apple and an orange, given by the hospital staff for lunch. Big scars are still visible on his face and he has trouble moving with the cast on his leg. "He still has shrapnel encrusted in his body and his leg was broken in the bombing", comments Kitba.

Khaled advises her on how to facilitate her nephew's recovery. "At this stage, we can't do much more than that. Ali is too young," explains the physiotherapist. "But as soon as the doctors will remove his cast, we'll provide him with physiotherapy sessions. It is essential if we want him to recover well."

Kitba already seems to treat Ali as a second mother. She listens carefully to what Khaled tells her. "When we'll leave the hospital, my nephew will come with us," she says with tears in her eyes.

"His future is in God's hands but my only wish is for him to be happy, just like for my own son. When he is old enough to understand, I will tell him what happened to his parents. And I want everybody to know their story, not only Ali."

⇨ The above information is reprinted with kind permission from Handicap International. Please visit www.handicap-international.org.uk for further information.

Child soldier recruits double in one year in Middle East and North Africa

Report claims 28 million children living in countries at war are now in need of humanitarian help as families struggle to cope amid the chaos and violence.

By Karen McVeigh

The number of children recruited to fight in conflicts across the Middle East and North Africa has more than doubled in a year, UN analysis has found. The huge increase in child soldiers in Syria, Yemen, Iraq and other countries follows years of ongoing violence, displacement and a lack of basic services, which has reduced the coping mechanisms of families, according to Unicef.

Almost one in five children across the region – 28 million in all – now need immediate humanitarian assistance. More than 90% of these children live in countries affected by conflict, and in some cases families are sending their children to fight.

"With no end in sight to these conflicts and with families' dwindling financial resources, many have no choice but to send their children to work or marry their daughters early," said Geert Cappelaere, Unicef's regional director. "The number of children affiliated with the fighting has more than doubled."

The agency said in the past it had witnessed children working as porters, guards or paramedics, but it was now seeing them take on more active roles, carrying guns, manning checkpoints and being trained as paid soldiers. The number of children actively recruited into fighting rose from 576 in 2014 to 1,168 in 2015, according to verified UN figures.

The situation in Yemen was particularly grave, with a fivefold increase in children recruited into armed conflict in 2015 compared with the previous year. Such numbers were likely to be an underestimate, Unicef said. Children were also being recruited as soldiers in Sudan and Libya.

Years of ongoing violence, displacement and a lack of basic services have hit children hardest and threaten to reverse child development gains, said Unicef. "Conflict continues to rob millions of girls and boys of their childhood," Cappelaere said. "Decades of progress are at a risk of being reversed across the Middle East and North Africa."

Civilian infrastructure – including hospitals and energy, water and sanitation facilities – has come under attack in countries including Yemen, Syria and Iraq. Millions of families have been forced to flee their homes, some of them repeatedly, and under fire, the agency said.

Last week, the UN reported that 1,700 children, some as young as ten, had been recruited to fight in the three-year conflict in Yemen. The deteriorating situation in the country is now the worst humanitarian crisis in the world, with almost 18.8 million people in need of aid and seven million on the brink of famine.

More than half of the country's health facilities are out of service, water facilities have been destroyed and more than 15 million children are in need of water and sanitation facilities. The country is in the grip of the world's worst cholera outbreak, with more than 610,000 suspected cases to date. More than 2,000 people have died from the highly contagious but curable bacterial infection since April this year, with thousands of new cases every day.

Inside Syria and in countries hosting refugees, such as Lebanon and Jordan, about 12 million Syrian children require humanitarian assistance, Unicef found. An estimated two million children live in hard to reach or besieged areas in Syria, which have received limited humanitarian assistance over the years.

In Iraq, more than five million children are in need of assistance as heavy fighting intensified recently in Tel Afar and in Mosul. They need food, shelter and education.

In the Gaza strip, an ongoing electricity crisis has reduced access to water by 30%. Cases of diarrhoea in children have doubled in three months, the UN agency said.

"Children in the Middle East and North Africa region have undergone unprecedented levels of violence and witnessed horrors that no one should witness. If violence and wars continue, the consequences – not only for the region but for the world as a whole – will be dire. World leaders must do much more to put an end to violence for the sake of boys and girls and their future," said Cappelaere.

Last week, Unicef figures showed how war was affecting children's chances in education. Conflicts in Iraq and Syria had resulted in an additional 3.4 million missing out on their schooling, bringing the number of out-of-school children across the Middle East and North Africa back to 2007's level of about 16 million.

11 September 2017

⇨ The above information is reprinted with kind permission from *The Guardian*. Please visit www.theguardian.com for further information.

"My wounds still hurt and I am very afraid": Yemen's civil war in the words of its forgotten children

"I have nightmares at night – I see aircraft hitting our house again and again," says six-year-old Noor.

As MPs prepare to debate the worsening humanitarian crisis in Yemen, the tragic suffering of some of the conflict's youngest victims has come to the fore.

Two years since the civil war began, at least 1,546 children have been killed and 2,450 maimed.

Nine-year-old Ali wears two hearing aids and barely speaks after an airstrike hit a building near his home in Sa'ada Governorate. The blast threw him from a window and he fell two storeys, before landing on his neck.

"Blood was coming out of Ali's ears and nose," his mother Enas said. "Blood was even coming out from his mouth… it was hard for him to even breathe."

She added: "We took shelter in a small ground room that was made from mud. It was the most horrible night of our lives. Ali was injured and we couldn't take him to the hospital – there were the sounds of the flying jets and missiles falling one after the other very close to our home."

Khalil and his sister Noor, aged nine and six, were peppered with shrapnel when an airstrike hit their home on New Year's Day. The attack killed their grandfather, three-year-old cousin and three guests.

Khalil has since stopped going to school and Noor is too afraid to leave the house.

"I was playing in the yard with my brother, and then we heard the missile coming towards us," Noor said, adding that she was "so scared", she kept her eyes closed.

"My wounds still hurt and I am very afraid when I hear aircraft overhead," she said. "I have nightmares at night – I see aircraft hitting our house again and again. My brother and I cannot sleep properly. Sometimes I wake up because I hear my brother Khalil shouting while he is asleep."

Leading charities believe all parties involved in the conflict – which has displaced more than three million people – are guilty of violating international law, with reports of homes, schools and hospitals being targeted.

The bloodshed started in March 2015 after an opposition offensive led by Houthi rebels drove the government out of the capital Sana'a, sparking an intervention by Saudi Arabia and its allies to support the internationally-recognised government.

More than 7,600 people have been killed so far in the fight for control between forces loyal to President Abdrabbuh Mansour Hadi and those allied to the rebels.

The UN human rights office said the Saudi-led air campaign, seeing rebel-controlled areas heavily bombarded, was responsible for 60 per cent of civilian deaths – almost 2,300 lives.

British-manufactured weapons, including cluster bombs, have been used in the strikes, despite calls by MPs to suspend sales to Saudi Arabia over war crimes allegations.

Peter Salisbury, a senior research fellow in the Middle East and North Africa programme at Chatham House, said Britain was the principal sponsor of a UN Security Council resolution used by Saudi Arabia to justify its intervention.

"The UK is also a huge arms supplier and provides a great deal of logistical support to Saudi forces," he told The Independent. "Arguably the UK has also given political coverage to the Saudis by preventing various resolutions and investigations from happening."

Save the Children is calling for the UK to ban arms sales to Saudi Arabia as the crisis rages. The charity also wishes to see an independent international inquiry into alleged violations of international humanitarian law.

"In this crisis children are not just being bombed – they are also being starved. The Saudi-led coalition is stopping vital supplies getting in by sea, while warring parties are detaining aid workers and obstructing deliveries by land," Save the Children's Interim Country Director for Yemen Grant Pritchard said.

"Millions of children and their families have no idea where their next meal is coming from, or where the next bomb will fall."

Tuesday's meeting will see MPs debate the motion: "That this House notes the worsening humanitarian crisis in Yemen; and calls upon the Government to take a lead in passing a resolution at the UN Security Council that would give effect to an immediate ceasefire in Yemen."

A landmark judgement to determine the legality of British arms transfers to Saudi Arabia is also expected to be announced in the near future.

27 March 2017

⇨ The above information is reprinted with kind permission from *The Independent*. Please visit www.independent.co.uk for further information.

Launch of new inquiry on protecting children in conflict

An international inquiry tasked with strengthening the framework for the protection of children in conflict and holding perpetrators of abuses to account was announced today. Speaking at the United Nations Headquarters in New York, the UN Special Envoy for Global Education and former UK Prime Minister Gordon Brown unveiled the Inquiry on Protecting Children in Conflict – which will aim to halt the widespread violation of children's rights in conflict zones.

The last year has seen an escalation in the war on children – from the sexual enslavement of children to the deliberate bombing of their schools – subjecting a generation of children to targeted violence and indiscriminate attacks. Crimes against children which should send shockwaves around the world are coming to be accepted as commonplace. In Syria, Iraq, South Sudan, Nigeria, Yemen, Afghanistan and elsewhere, the international laws and human rights provisions developed in the 20th century are being violated at an alarming rate and the institutions designed to defend these norms are failing to provide protection. This calls for a review of the existing laws and enforcement mechanisms that are supposed to protect children.

The new Inquiry on Protecting Children in Conflict will undertake this review with the aim of helping to stem the tide of violations of children's rights. Building on the work of the Special Representative of the Secretary-General for Children and Armed Conflict, the Inquiry will consider the adequacy and effectiveness of existing laws and enforcement mechanisms – and consider whether there are new laws or procedures that may enhance the protection of children. The final report will be published and submitted to UN Secretary-General António Guterres in December 2017.

The Inquiry, which is supported by Save the Children UK and Theirworld, comprises two groups:

⇨ A legal panel, led by Shaheed Fatima QC of Blackstone Chambers, London, bringing together lawyers with a broad range of expertise, which will consider the adequacy and effectiveness of existing laws and enforcement mechanisms and possible reforms aimed at enhancing the protection of children.

⇨ An advisory panel of globally influential policy-makers, thinkers and activists which will receive the report of the legal panel and consider its recommendations. In doing so, they will take into account the role of foreign policy and soft power in the protection of children and ways of building a large and diverse coalition of states and national leaders in support of this agenda.

Gordon Brown, who will act as Chair of the Inquiry, said:

"We must not allow ourselves to become inured to the senseless acts of violence befalling children in conflict zones, Syria being a prime example. Moral lines – such as the recent Idlib gas attack – have been crossed in Syria. Other less visible atrocities include the deliberate bombing of children in their schools, as happened in the same Syrian province on 26 October last year, the abuse and trafficking of children, the militarisation of schools and the use of child militias.

"Not since 1945 have so many children been subjected to such widespread violations of their human rights in conflict zones – in Yemen, where schools have become instruments of war and children used as human shields; in Iraq, where girls are being systematically raped; and across the Middle East, Africa and Asia where thousands of girls are being abducted and sold as slaves. The latest outrage is Boko Haram's use of children as suicide bombers.

"Eglantyne Jebb, the founder of Save the Children, once said that the only international language we understand is the cry of the child. But J.K. Rowling is probably nearer the truth when she said that children may be seen but are usually not heard. For it is questionable whether existing international legal norms and institutions provide adequate accountability for the widespread violations of children's rights.

"In 1996, Graça Machel's path-breaking report on the *Impact of Armed Conflict on Children* led to the creation of a UN Special Representative and an annual report to the Security Council that names and shames states and non-state actors responsible for grave violations against children in war zones. But 20 years on, it is time to revisit and ask what more can be done – practically and effectively – when moral lines are crossed.

"The new Inquiry on Protecting Children in Conflict will consider what may be done to strengthen the current framework for the protection of children and to hold the perpetrators of atrocities to account. Only when international law is robust enough – substantively and procedurally – to secure accountability for children's rights, will we have done all in our power to ensure that no child of God will ever again suffer the horrors of Syria."

19 April 2017

⇨ The above information is reprinted with kind permission from Save the Children. Please visit www.savethechildren.org.uk for further information.

Key facts

⇨ North Korea has conducted its sixth nuclear device test, and based on what we know so far it looks like by far the biggest yet. Seismic readings detected the blast via a 6.3 magnitude earthquake, and Norway's NORSAR seismological observatory suggested the explosive yield would translate to a massive 120 kilotons (page 8)

⇨ North Korea has produced a number of nuclear warheads and is developing ballistic missiles capable of delivering them around the world (page 9)

⇨ Since 1975, landmines have killed or maimed more than a million people, 80 per cent of them civilians. The disabilities caused by mines are devastating. And, in countries where access to physiotherapy and prostheses is poor – that is, most countries where landmines exist – the lifelong impact on wellbeing is extreme (page 11)

⇨ ISIS is a direct outgrowth of al-Qaeda in Iraq that grew out of our invasion in 2003, which is an example of unintended consequences (page 14)

⇨ According to 70% of the British public, the UK Government should not be promoting the sales of British military equipment to foreign governments that have poor human rights records (page 17)

⇨ When it comes to non-democratic countries, the level of opposition is similar: 60% think that it is wrong for the UK Government to promote the sale of British military equipment to foreign countries that are not democracies, such as dictatorships, military regimes and unstable states (page 17)

⇨ More than a hundred suicide bombers have hurled themselves at Iraqi troops since the Mosul offensive began on 17 October, a rate of self-annihilation never before seen even by the extreme standards of Isil (page 22)

⇨ In 2016 there were over three million people in Iraq who had been forced to flee their homes due to the violence and destruction caused by Isis and other internal sectarian conflicts.

⇨ On 25 March 2015, an international coalition led by Saudi Arabia launched air strikes against the Huthi armed group in Yemen sparking a full-blown armed conflict (page 24)

• Over the following two years, the conflict has spread and fighting has engulfed the entire country. Horrific human rights abuses, as well as war crimes, are being committed throughout the country causing unbearable suffering for civilians (page 24)

• Approximately 18.8 million Yemenis today rely on humanitarian assistance in order to survive (page 24)

• Amnesty International has documented 34 air strikes across six different governorates (Sana'a, Sa'da, Hajjah, Hodeidah, Ta'iz and Lahj) by the Saudi Arabia-led coalition that appear to have violated international humanitarian law – the rules that apply during a conflict which are sometimes known as the "laws of war" – resulting in 494 civilian deaths (including at least 148 children) and 359 civilian injuries. These have included attacks that appear to have deliberately targeted civilians and civilian objects such as hospitals, schools, markets and mosques, which may amount to war crimes (page 25)

⇨ Millions of children are on the move across international borders – fleeing violence and conflict, disaster or poverty, in pursuit of a better life (page 26)

• On the dangerous Central Mediterranean Sea passage from North Africa to Europe, 92 per cent of children who arrived in Italy in 2016 and the first two months of 2017 were unaccompanied, up from 75 per cent in 2015. At least 300,000 unaccompanied and separated children moving across borders were registered in 80 countries in 2015–2016 – a near fivefold increase from 66,000 in 2010–2011 (page 26)

• Since 1990, the number of international child migrants has grown along with the global population, with the share of migrants among the world's children remaining stable (page 28)

⇨ Nearly a quarter of the world's school-aged children – 462 million – now live in countries affected by crisis.

⇨ Over the past 40 years, international law has developed to better protect children from military exploitation (page 30)

• In 1977, the Additional Protocols to the 1949 Geneva Conventions prohibited the military recruitment and use of children under the age of 15, which is now recognised as a war crime under the Rome Statute of the International Criminal Court (2002). It applies to both government-controlled armed forces and non-state armed groups (page 30)

• The number of children recruited to fight in conflicts across the Middle East and North Africa has more than doubled in a year (page 37)

• UNICEF figures showed how war was affecting children's chances in education. Conflicts in Iraq and Syria had resulted in an additional 3.4 million missing out on their schooling, bringing the number of out-of-school children across the Middle East and North Africa back to 2007's level of about 16 million (page 37)

Arms Trade Treaty (ATT)

The purpose of the Arms Trade Treaty (ATT) is to monitor and control the trading of weapons (arms) more closely; ensuring that weapons are traded more responsibly and preventing arms being supplied to people who abuse human rights law.

Chemical weapons

Weapons that use deadly chemicals to hurt, maim and kill their targets. These chemicals can be in the form of a gas, a liquid or a solid and can be used over a wide area.

Humanitarian intervention

When a state uses military force against another state whose military action is violating citizens' human rights.

Internal conflict

Conflict that takes place within a state, between government forces and one or more organised groups. Or between these groups themselves.

Internal displacement

When people are forced to flee – whether due to natural disasters, chemical/nuclear disasters, famine, development projects or conflict – and remain within the borders of their country.

International human rights law

International humanitarian law (IHL) is a set of rules which seek to protect people who are not participating in armed conflict, like civilians and wounded, sick or shipwrecked members of the armed forces. It also restricts the means and methods of warfare. Also known as the law of war or the law of armed conflict, the best known of these rules are the four Geneva Conventions of 1949.

International Humanitarian Law (IHL)

A set of rules and principles that govern armed conflict. IHL protects refugees from States that are involved in armed conflict.

Landmine

An explosive device that is hidden just beneath the ground and goes off when someone passes near or over the device. Landmines have been increasingly used around the world because they do not cost much to make yet they cause a lot of damage. They can remain hidden for years or even decades, which poses a risk to civilians or aid workers long after a conflict has ended.

Nuclear weapon

An explosive device that has enormous destructive power and releases a vast amount of energy. Even a small nuclear weapon has the power to wipe out a city. Also known as Weapons of Mass Destruction (WMD)

Peacekeeping

Actively maintaining peaceful relations between nations.

Refugee

A person who has left their home country and cannot return because they fear that they will be persecuted on the grounds of race, religion, nationality, political affiliation or social group. In the UK, a person is officially known as a refugee when they claim asylum and this claim is accepted by the Government.

Responsibility to Protect

The Responsibility to Protect (RtoP or R2P) is in place to prevent and stop genocide, war crimes, ethnic cleansing and crimes against humanity. The Responsibility to Protect is not a law, but rather a political commitment to guide states in protecting populations from these crimes and violations.

War

Armed conflict between different countries/groups/states.

Assignments

Brainstorming

⇨ As a class, brainstorm what you know about conflict in other countries

- what do you understand by the term 'Global Conflict'?

- what does the term 'nuclear' mean?

- what is a landmine?

- where is Syria?

Research

⇨ Conduct a questionnaire amongst your friends, family and peers to find out their view on Nuclear Warfare. Ask at least five different questions, including their views on the recent threat from North Korea. Write an article showing your findings and share it with the rest of the class.

⇨ In pairs, research the sale of arms to Saudi Arabia. You should consider the reasons we sell arms to other countries. Write a report on your findings.

⇨ In small groups, find out as much as you can about the Red Cross and their role in conflict areas. Which countries do they work in? Prepare a bullet point list and share your findings with the other groups in the class.

⇨ Who are ISIS? Do some research about them and write a report. Share this with your class.

⇨ Do some research into suicide bombings. Try to find out the reasons someone might be prepared to commit an act like this and in doing so take their own life. Write a two-page essay on the subject.

Design

⇨ Imagine that you work for a charity that is compaigning against the recruitment of child soldiers. Create a poster that could be displayed in public places such as tube stations that will highlight your cause.

⇨ Choose an article from the book and design your own illustration highlighting its key points.

⇨ Read the article on page 20 and design your own 'payment method'. It could be a card, coin or any other method you can think of.

⇨ Design a robot which can be used to clear landmines. You should produce a drawing of the robot and share this with the other members of your class.

⇨ Design a poster highlighting the plight of child refugees. It should raise awareness of the difficulties they face.

Oral

⇨ As a class, discuss the plight of school-age children living in conflict areas. How does their life differ from yours? What issues do they experience in their everyday lives?

⇨ HMS *Belfast* is a new warship which has been produced along with two Type 26 frigates at a cost of £178 billion. (see page 12). Split the class into two groups each taking a different viewpoint and discuss if you think we should spend these large amounts on defence. Take into account the shortages in, for example, the NHS and if the money could be put to better use.

⇨ We see every day in the media stories about child refugees fleeing from conflict areas. Many of them travel alone without any adult supervision. As a class, discuss this subject and the problems they might face.

Reading/Writing

⇨ Read the article "My wounds still hurt and I am very afraid" on page 38. Write a letter to an MP telling them you are concerned about the lives these children are living and explaining why this issue matters to you. Ask them to raise the subject of the humanitarian crisis in the Yemen when next in Parliament.

⇨ Write a definition of 'The British Arms Trade'.

⇨ Write a definition of 'A Child Soldier'.

⇨ Read the article 'Islamic state launches unprecendented wave of suicide bombers to try to defend Mosul' and write an article for your school newspaper based on this article. It should raise awareness of this issue.

⇨ Read the article on page 29 relating to school-age children who live in crisis-hit countries. Write an essay on this subject. You should write at least two sides of A4.

Acknowledgements

The publisher is grateful for permission to reproduce the material in this book. While every care has been taken to trace and acknowledge copyright, the publisher tenders its apology for any accidental infringement or where copyright has proved untraceable. The publisher would be pleased to come to a suitable arrangement in any such case with the rightful owner.

Images

All images courtesy of iStock except pages 6, 7, 8, and 22: Pixabay.

Icons

Icons on pages 26, 27 and 28 were made by Freepik from www.flaticon.com.

Illustrations

Don Hatcher: pages 14 & 30. Simon Kneebone: pages 11 & 18. Angelo Madrid: pages 5 & 34.

Additional acknowledgements

With thanks to the Independence team: Shelley Baldry, Sandra Dennis, Jackie Staines and Jan Sunderland.

Tina Brand

Cambridge, January 2018